Series/Number 07-135

D0705993

INTERACTION EFFECTS IN LOGISTIC REGRESSION

JAMES JACCARD
Department of Psychology, University at Albany,
State University of New York

SAGE PUBLICATIONS
International Educational and Professional Publisher
Thousand Oaks London New Delhi

For information:

Sage Publications, Inc.
2455 Teller Road
Thousand Oaks, California 91320
E-mail: order@sagepub.com

Sage Publications Ltd.
6 Bonhill Street
London EC2A 4PU
United Kingdom

Sage Publications India Pvt. Ltd.
M-32 Market
Greater Kailash I
New Delhi 110 048 India

Printed in the United States of America

0-7619-2207-5 (pbk.: acid-free paper)

This book is printed on acid-free paper.

03 04 05 10 9 8 7 6 5 4 3

Acquiring Editor:	C. Deborah Laughton
Editorial Assistant:	Eileen Carr
Production Editor:	Denise Santoyo
Production Assistant:	Cindy Bear
Typesetter:	Technical Typesetting Inc.

When citing a university paper, please use the proper form. Remember to cite the Sage University Paper series title and include paper number. One of the following formats can be adapted (depending on the style manual used):

(1) JACCARD, J. (2001) *Interaction Effects in Logistic Regression.* Sage University Papers Series on Quantitative Applications in the Social Sciences, 07-135. Thousand Oaks, CA: Sage.

OR

(2) Jaccard, J. (2001). *Interaction Effects in Logistic Regression.* (Sage University Papers Series on Quantitative Applications in the Social Sciences, series no. 07-135). Thousand Oaks, CA: Sage.

CONTENTS

SERIES EDITOR'S INTRODUCTION

The basics of modeling interaction effects in the regression analysis of nonexperimental data are now widely understood. If the effect of X on Y varies with the value of Z, then there is interaction. The appropriate model is not the usual $Y = a + bX + cZ$. Better, it should be $Y = a + bX + cZ + d(XZ)$. The inclusion of the multiplicative, or product term, (XZ), registers the interaction effect through estimation of the coefficient, d. Take a simple example, where Y = income in dollars, X = education in years, and Z = gender (1 = male, 0 = female). The interaction hypothesis is that the impact of education on income depends on gender. The prediction equation simplifies for males to $Y = (a + c) + (b + d)X$ and for females to $Y = a + bX$. If the coefficient, d, in the general equation tests positive and significant, then the inference is that increases in education have a bigger income effect for males than for females. In the parlance of Dr. Jaccard, the impact of X, the *focal* independent variable, is moderated by the *moderator* variable, Z.

The basics, as well as many subtleties, of interaction effects in multiple regression were explicated by Dr. Jaccard in his first series monograph on the subject, appearing in 1990 (Jaccard, Turrisi, and Wan, *Interaction Effects in Multiple Regression*, No. 72). That work helped popularize their use. Since that monograph, he has explored interaction effects in LISREL and in factorial ANOVA (see, respectively, Jaccard and Wan, *LISREL Approaches to Interaction Effects in Multiple Regression*, No. 114; Jaccard, *Interaction Effects in Factorial Analysis of Variance* No. 118). The monograph at hand, with applications for the logistic regression case, clinches his title as the leading expert on interaction effects. This contribution is of theoretical and practical importance. While logistic regression is much in vogue, precious little is known about modeling interaction within that framework. In some ways, the current level of understanding takes us back to the 1960s, by shunning the construction of product terms on the right-hand side of the equation. That state of affairs will be changed with this effort.

At all points in the exposition, the emphasis is on interpretation. He begins with a review of the usual meaning of logistic effects in terms of probability, odds, and log odds. In logistic regression, like ordinary regression, interactions are normally modeled by the creation of product terms. The first, and most simple, example is of a two-way interaction between two qualitative independent variables. A psychologist investigating teenage sexuality has a dichotomous Y (1 = has engaged in sex, 0 = otherwise), with two predictors, gender (G, where 1 = male, 0 = female) and employment status of mother (two dummies F = full-time or not, P = part-time or not). In the logistic regression, the dependent variable is the log odds of Y, the independent variables are G, F, and P, and the product terms are GF and GP. Say the hypothesis is that employment status moderates the effect of gender. The logistic coefficient for GP (whose exponent equals the odds ratio for gender for teens of part-time mothers divided by the odds ratio for gender for teens of unemployed mothers) is statistically significant, suggesting that there is an interaction. After examining this two-way interaction, the author goes on to illustrate a three-way interaction, where the dependent variable is return of a mail survey, and predictors are three qualitative variables—money reward, survey length, and topic importance—in a $2 \times 2 \times 2$ factorial design.

Subsequent chapters deal with coefficient interpretation in the more complex cases of interactions between qualitative and quantitative predictors, between quantitative predictors, and between different predictors when the dependent variable is multinomial. To illustrate the last, Dr. Jaccard posits a child psychologist studying three different attachment patterns to a caretaker, as a function of home environment and maternal affect. These data were analyzed with the multinomial logistic regression program of SPSS. As noted, the necessary computer software for the analysis of interaction effects in a logistic regression context is readily available. Thus, the real obstacle to work here has been interpretation difficulties, which this step-by-step guide aims to overcome.

—*Michael S. Lewis-Beck*
Series Editor

PREFACE

This monograph is an introduction to the analysis of interaction effects in logistic regression by means of product terms. The focus is on the interpretation of the coefficients of interactive logistic models for a wide range of scenarios encountered in the research literature. I assume that the reader is familiar with the basics of logistic regression and the concept of hierarchical logistic regression. The monograph is neither a technical nor an advanced exposition of this complex topic. My goal is to present a nontechnical, introductory orientation to the interpretation of logistic coefficients in simple product term models when the product terms have been defined to explore certain forms of interaction. Although many books on logistic regression discuss general strategies for testing interactions, few provide readers with the tools to interpret and understand the meaning of coefficients in equations with product terms. This monograph will fill this void. The monograph is oriented toward the applied researcher with rudimentary background in multiple regression and logistic regression. I have explicitly avoided complex formulas that can be intimidating to the applied researcher. As an alternative, I have provided the reader with simple (but cumbersome) computer-based heuristics that permit the simple calculation of parameter estimates and estimated standard errors that will typically be of interest. Results of examples are reported to four decimals to minimize rounding error, although same minor rounding inconsistencies still manifest themselves on occasion.

I would like to acknowledge the useful comments of the reviewers, Alfred DeMaris from the Department of Sociology, Bowling Green State University, Bowling Green, OH 43403-0231, Jacques Hagenaars from the Faculty of Social and Behavioural Sciences, Tilburg University, NL-5000 LE Tilburg, The Netherlands, and Scott Menard from the Institute of Behavioral Science, University of Colorado, Boulder, CO 80309, Dimitri Liakhovitski, Paul Goren, Glenn Deane, Richard Alba, and the continued support of the series editor, Michael Lewis-Beck. I am grateful for the time and effort they put into this project.

For the best interactions ever,
this book is dedicated to
Liliana
and
Sarita

INTERACTION EFFECTS IN LOGISTIC REGRESSION

JAMES JACCARD
Department of Psychology, University at Albany, State University of New York

1. INTRODUCTION

Interaction effects are becoming more common in social science theory and with their increasing popularity, there has been renewed interest in developing analytic methods that can effectively characterize the nature of interactions in a given set of data. These methods have included interaction analysis in traditional multiple regression and analysis of variance as well as methods for analyzing interactions in structural equation models (e.g., Jaccard, Turrisi, & Wan, 1990; Jaccard & Wan, 1996, Jaccard, 1998). The present monograph focuses on the analysis of interaction effects using product terms in logistic regression. There are numerous excellent introductory treatments of logistic regression (Agresti, 1996; Allison, 1999b; Long, 1997; Menard, 1995), and it is assumed that the reader is already familiar with the fundamentals of this analytic technique. Although many texts discuss the use of product terms to analyze interactions in logistic regression in general terms, few probe the meaning of the coefficients associated with product terms and how the presence of product terms alters the interpretation of other coefficients within the equation. This monograph is an introduction to interpretational issues in the analysis of interaction effects in logistic regression. It is divided into six chapters. The present chapter introduces the concept of odds, presents the logistic regression model without interaction terms, discusses the meaning of coefficients within the model, elaborates the effects of selected transformations on the coefficients, and formally defines an interaction effect in conceptual terms. Chapter 2 considers the analysis of interactions when the predictor variables of interest are categorical in nature. Chapter 3 considers the case where the predictors are a mixture of categorical and quantitative/continuous variables. Chapter 4 addresses the case where the predictors are all quantitative/continuous. Chapter 5 extends the material of the previous chapters to the case of ordinal regression and multinomial logistic regression. The final chapter focuses on miscellaneous issues associated with effective interaction analysis.

Probabilities and Odds

Consider a dichotomous variable, Y, which is scored 1 if a person says he or she will vote for a given piece of legislation and 0 if the person says he or she will not. For a population of individuals, the mean of Y is denoted by μ. This mean equals the proportion of individuals who have a score of 1 (i.e., the proportion of individuals who say they will vote for the legislation). It also represents the probability that an individual from the population will vote for the legislation [i.e., $\mu = P(Y = 1)$]. If $\mu = 0.67$, then the probability of a person voting for the legislation is 0.67 or, stated another way, about two thirds of the population favor the legislation. Although a probability is one useful statistic for characterizing this scenario, an alternative approach uses the concept of odds instead of probability. If P is the probability of an event (e.g., the probability that $Y = 1$), then the odds of that event are

$$\text{Odds} = P/(1 - P). \qquad [1]$$

In the above example, the odds of voting for the legislation are $0.67/0.33 = 2.0$. The probability of voting for the legislation is twice the size of the probability of not voting for the legislation. This is the essence of an odds. It compares two probabilities by forming the ratio of the probabilities. If the probabilities are equal, the odds are 1.0. As the probabilities diverge, the odds diverge from 1.00. Every probability has associated with it a unique value of odds. For example, consider the following:

Probability	Associated Odds
0.25	0.33
0.33	0.50
0.50	1.00
0.67	2.00
0.75	3.00

An odds of 0.33 means that the probability of voting for the legislation is one third that of the probability of not voting for it. An odds of 1.00 means that the probability of voting for the legislation is the same as the probability of not voting for it. An odds of 3.00 means that the probability of voting for the legislation is 3 times larger than the probability of not voting for it. Many social scientists characterize events using odds rather than probabilities. Note that for a dichotomous variable with scores of 1 and 0, the odds of a score of 1 is $\mu/(1-\mu)$, because μ is the probability of a score of 1. Just as a probability can be converted to an odds, so can an odds be converted to a probability:

$$\text{Probability} = \frac{\text{odds}}{(1+\text{odds})}. \qquad [2]$$

Most researchers who use logistic regression rely on the concept of odds to impose theoretical meaning on the results of the analysis. However, it is possible to make statements using probabilities by taking advantage of Equation 2. Complications arise when doing so, and our focus in this monograph will be on the interpretation of results in terms of odds.

The Logistic Regression Model

The logistic model is similar in form to the traditional linear regression model that is widely used in the social sciences in that it uses the equation form $Y = \alpha + \beta_1 X_1 + \beta_2 X_2 + \cdots + \beta_k X_k$. However, important differences exist. These differences are best understood when both models are described as special cases of the generalized linear model (McCullagh & Nelder, 1989). The generalized linear model has three components, a random component, a systematic component, and a link component (Agresti, 1996). The *random component* refers to the outcome variable, Y, and the probability distribution that is associated with it. In traditional regression analysis, Y is a continuous variable and is assumed to be normally distributed. In classic logistic regression, Y is dichotomous in character and the underlying probability distribution is binomial in form. The *systematic component* refers to the predictor variables and how they are combined for purposes of building an explanatory model. In both traditional linear regression and logistic regression, the systematic component has the form

$$\alpha + \beta_1 X_1 + \beta_2 X_2 + \cdots + \beta_k X_k$$

where α is an intercept, the β are regression coefficients, and the X are the predictors. This expression is often called a *linear predictor*. Note that a given X can be a combination of other predictors [e.g., $X_3 = (X_1)(X_2)$] so that interactions and curvilinear effects can be accommodated in the model. The *link component* specifies how the mean of Y, $\mu = E(Y)$, is related to the linear predictor. The mean can be modeled directly or, instead, some monotonic function of the mean can be modeled. A general expression of this is

$$g(\mu) = \alpha + \beta_1 X_1 + \beta_2 X_2 + \cdots + \beta_k X_k \qquad [3]$$

where the function $g(\mu)$ represents some function of the mean. It is called the link function. When the mean is modeled directly, the link function is said to be an identity, and interest is in specifying how the mean of Y changes for different profiles of the predictor variables. For example, how does the mean on Y change when X_1 changes by 1 unit and all other predictor variables are held constant? This is the focus of traditional linear regression. By contrast, logistic regression does not model the mean of Y directly. Rather it models the mean as transformed by a *logit link*, which is defined as $\ln(\mu/(1-\mu))$. Note that for a dichotomous Y variable with values of 1 and 0, the model focuses on how the natural log of the odds that $Y = 1$ varies as a function of the linear predictor $\alpha + \beta_1 X_1 + \beta_2 X_2 + \cdots + \beta_k X_k$. There are many statistical advantages to modeling the logit link rather than the mean directly when Y is dichotomous in nature. Most of these derive from the fact that the underlying statistical theory is mathematically tractable for the case of the logit link. In the remainder of this monograph, we use the following terminology (Agresti, 1996): For a dichotomous variable, Y, that is scored 1 and 0, the probability that $Y = 1$ is denoted as π. The term $\text{logit}(\pi)$ refers to the logit function of this probability and equals the natural log of $\pi/(1-\pi)$. The model describing the relationship between $\text{logit}(\pi)$ and a set of predictors X is

$$\text{logit}(\pi) = \alpha + \beta_1 X_1 + \beta_2 X_2 + \cdots + \beta_k X_k. \qquad [4]$$

Equation 4 describes the log odds that $Y = 1$ as a function of the values of the predictors, X. The focus of this monograph is on specifying meaningful interpretations of α and β in the context of applied data analytic situations using logistic regression models that include product terms to represent interaction effects. As noted, Equation 4 is similar to that of the traditional linear regression model. It should not be surprising, then, that many of the same considerations that are involved in effective interaction analysis in traditional ordinary least squares regression are also relevant in logistic regression.

Categorical Predictors and Dummy Variables

Logistic regression analysis often includes categorical variables as predictors, such as gender, ethnicity, and religious affiliation. Such variables are represented in the equation using dummy variables. A dummy variable is a variable that is created by the analyst to represent group membership on a variable. For example, in the case of gender, we can create a dummy variable and assign a 1 to all males and a 0 to all females. This method of scoring is called "dummy coding" or "indicator coding" and involves assigning a 1 to all members of one group and a 0 to everyone else. When a qualitative variable has more than two levels, it is necessary to specify more than one dummy variable to capture membership in the different groups. In general, one needs $m - 1$ dummy variables, where m is the number of levels of the variable. Suppose we had as a predictor variable a person's party affiliation that could take on three values, Democrat, Republican, or Independent. In this case, we need $3 - 1 = 2$ dummy variables to represent party affiliation. For the first dummy variable, D_D, we assign all Democrats a 1 and everyone else a 0. For the second dummy variable, D_R, we assign all Republicans a 1 and everyone else a 0. Although we could create a third dummy variable for Independents and assign them a 1 and everyone else a 0, such a variable is completely redundant with the other two dummy variables. Once we know whether someone is a Democrat or whether someone is a Republican (by means of the first two dummy variables), we know whether he or she is an Independent. The reasoning behind this is more evident if one considers a dummy variable for gender. We create a single dummy variable to discriminate the two groups whereby males are assigned a score of 1 and females a score of 0. If we create a second dummy variable that assigns a score of 1 to females and a score of 0 to males, it is perfectly negatively correlated with the first dummy variable and, hence, redundant. With dummy coding, the group that does not receive a 1 on any of the dummy variables is called the *reference group* for that variable. In the examples above, the reference group for gender is females and for party affiliation the reference group is Independents. The choice of which group is the reference group is arbitrary from a statistical point of view.

There are different ways in which scores can be assigned to a dummy variable. As noted, we used a method called "dummy" or "indicator" scoring that relies on 1's and 0's. Hardy (1993) discusses the logic of different coding schemes. We make use of dummy variables in later sections, and all of our statements about the interpretation of coefficients associated with dummy variables assume dummy coding. For a discussion of interpretations under alternative coding schemes, see Hosmer and Lemeshow (1989).

Predicted Values in Logistic Regression

Suppose a set of data are analyzed in which votes for or against a piece of legislation are predicted from gender and a measure of ideology that reflects general attitudes about conservatism-liberalism. The ideology measure ranges from −3 to +3 with 0 representing a neutral point, increasingly negative scores representing greater levels of conservatism, and increasingly positive scores representing greater levels of liberalism. Gender is represented by a dummy variable, with males scored 1 and females scored 0. The outcome measure is scored 1 if the individual endorses the legislation and 0 if the individual opposes it. Suppose that the analysis yielded the following logistic equation:

$$\text{logit}(\pi) = 1.555 + -1.712 \text{ gender} + -0.513 \text{ ideology}. \qquad [5]$$

We can calculate a predicted value of $\text{logit}(\pi)$ for any given profile of predictor variables by substituting the values for the predictors into the equation. For example, the predicted log odds for males who have ideology scores of +2 is

$$\text{logit}(\pi) = 1.555 + -1.712(1) + -0.513(2) = -1.183.$$

We can convert this log odds to an odds by taking the exponent of this value, which yields $\exp(-1.183) = 0.306$.[1] The predicted odds of voting in favor of the legislation is low for people with this particular profile and reveals that the probability of voting for the legislation is about one third that of voting against it. What are the predicted odds for males who have an ideology score of −2? By substitution, we obtain

$$\text{logit}(\pi) = 1.555 + -1.712(1) + -0.513(-2) = 0.869,$$

and the exponent of 0.869 is 2.384. For males with ideology scores of −2, the odds of voting in favor of the legislation is 2.384. Stated another way, the probability of voting for the legislation is over twice as large as the probability of voting against it.

Interpretation of Coefficients

The preceding material allows us to set the stage for the interpretation of the coefficients in Equations 4 and 5. The intercept term, α, is the predicted log odds when all the predictor variables equal 0. For females (who have a score of 0 on gender) with ideology scores of 0, the predicted log odds of voting for the legislation is 1.555 and the odds of voting for the legislation is the exponent of this, 4.735. For females with ideology scores of 0, it is almost 5 times more likely that they will vote for the legislation than vote against it.

The meaning of the coefficient for a dummy variable, such as gender, can be made explicit by calculating the predicted odds of voting for the legislation for males and also for females at some arbitrarily chosen value of ideology. For the sake of simplicity, we will set ideology to a value of 0. The predicted log odds for males and females are

Males: $\text{logit}(\pi) = 1.555 + -1.712(1) + -0.513(0) = -0.157$

Females: $\text{logit}(\pi) = 1.555 + -1.712(0) + -0.513(0) = 1.555,$

which yields a predicted odds for males of $\exp(-0.157) = 0.855$ and a predicted odds for females of $\exp(1.555) = 4.735$. A formal way of contrasting these two odds is to form an *odds ratio* in which the odds for one group is divided by the odds for the other group,

$$\text{OR for gender} = \frac{\text{odds for males}}{\text{odds for females}} = \frac{0.855}{4.735} = 0.1805,$$

where OR stands for "odds ratio." If the two odds are identical, then the odds ratio will equal 1.0. As the odds for one group deviate from the odds for the other group, the odds ratio will deviate from 1.0. In this case, the predicted odds for males are about one fifth the value of the predicted odds for females (more technically, they are 0.1805 the value of the odds for females), suggesting that males are much less likely to vote for the legislation than females. The value for this odds ratio, 0.1805, would be obtained no matter what value we held ideology constant at in the equation. To be sure, the value of the predicted odds for males and females would change if ideology is held constant at a different value (e.g., +2), but the *ratio* of the odds for males divided by females would not. It would always equal 0.1805. This will not necessarily be true in models that include interaction terms.

From Equation 5, the coefficient for gender was −1.712. If we calculate the exponent of the coefficient, we obtain $\exp(-1.712) = 0.1805$, which turns out to be the value of the odds ratio. *For a dummy variable with dummy coding, the exponent of the logistic coefficient will equal an odds ratio in which the predicted odds for the group scored 1 on the dummy variable is divided by the predicted odds for the reference group, holding constant all other predictor variables in the equation.*

We can use the same logic to develop the meaning of the coefficient for ideology. We hold gender constant at an arbitrary value (say 0) and then calculate the predicted log odds and the odds of voting in favor of the legislation at the different values of ideology:

Ideology Score	Predicted Log Odds	Predicted Odds
+3	0.016	1.017
+2	0.529	1.697
+1	1.042	2.835
0	1.555	4.735
−1	2.068	7.909
−2	2.581	13.210
−3	3.094	22.065

Although it may not be apparent, there is a systematic trend in the predicted odds. Every time ideology increases by 1 unit, the predicted odds change by a multiplicative factor of 0.599. For example, when the ideology score is −3, the predicted odds are 22.065. When the ideology score increases by 1 unit to −2, the predicted odds become (22.065)(0.599) = 13.210. When the ideology score is +1, the predicted odds are 2.835. When the ideology score increases by 1 unit to +2, the predicted odds become (2.835)(0.599) = 1.697. This trend reveals itself no matter what value we hold gender constant at. Again, the values of the predicted odds change when gender is held constant at a different value, but the multiplicative factor is still 0.599. This also will not necessarily be the case for models with interaction effects.

Examine the logistic coefficient for ideology in Equation 5. It equals −0.513. If we calculate the exponent of the coefficient, we obtain exp(−0.513) = 0.599, the value of the multiplicative factor. *For a quantitative/continuous variable, the exponent of the logistic coefficient equals a multiplicative factor by which the predicted odds change given a 1 unit increase in the predictor variable, holding constant all other predictor variables in the equation.* If the exponent of the coefficient is equal to 1.0, then changes in the predictor have no effect on the predicted odds. If the exponent of the coefficient is greater than 1.0, then an increase in the predictor will yield an increase in the predicted odds. If the exponent of the coefficient is less than 1.0, then an increase in the value of the predictor will yield a decrease in the predicted odds.

The "multiplying factor" identified for continuous/quantitative predictors is referred to by some researchers as an odds ratio because it is the result that one obtains when one divides the predicted odds at one value of the predictor by the predicted odds at that same value minus 1. The multiplying factor is indeed an odds ratio, but we will refer to it for continuous variables as a "multiplying factor," largely for pedagogical reasons.

Probabilities, Odds, and Log Odds Revisited

As noted earlier, every probability has associated with it an odds that can also be converted to log odds for analysis in logistic regression. Consider the following probabilities and their associated odds and log odds:

Probability	Odds	Log Odds
0.100	0.111	−2.197
0.200	0.250	−1.386
0.300	0.428	−0.847
0.400	0.667	−0.405
0.500	1.000	0.000
0.600	1.500	0.405
0.700	2.333	0.847
0.800	4.000	1.386
0.900	9.000	2.197

Probabilities range from 0 to 1.00, odds range from 0 to infinity, and log odds range from minus infinity to plus infinity. Probabilities less than 0.50 are associated with odds that are less than 1.0 and log odds that are negative. Probabilities that are greater than 0.50 are associated with odds that are greater than 1.0 and log odds that are positive. The fact that log odds are not bounded by 1 or 0 (as is the case with probabilities or odds) is a characteristic that makes log odds more amenable to a satisfactory underlying statistical theory in logistic regression. However, most social scientists find log odds to be counterintuitive and difficult to interpret and prefer instead to focus on odds. This gap typically has been bridged by applying the general linear model to log odds (thereby allowing us to invoke well-developed statistical theory that is tied to the well-known general linear model) and then transforming the log-based parameters to odds-based parameters by taking the antilogs of them. The effect of such transformations is nontrivial. Whereas log odds-based coefficients for dummy variables reflect differences in predicted log odds for two groups, the antilog transforms of the coefficients reflect the ratios of the predicted odds. Whereas log odds-based coefficients for continuous variables reflect how many log odds units the outcome variable is predicted to change given a 1 unit change in a predictor, the transformed coefficient reflects a multiplying constant by which the predicted odds change given a 1 unit change in the predictor. A focus on log odds is advantageous not only because of the elegance of the underlying statistical theory but also because it permits us to stay in the familiar terrain of the general linear model with the traditional interpretation of slopes and intercepts. For interaction models, it permits us to take the same general principles for analyzing interactions in traditional regression analysis and apply them directly to log odds based models. However, the intuitive appeal of odds and odds ratios results in the vast majority of social science research being reported in these terms rather than that of log odds. The focus of this monograph is on odds and odds ratios, accordingly.

Transformations of the Predictor Variables

It is possible to perform algebraic manipulations on the predictor variables prior to performing a logistic analysis to force the coefficients to reflect parameters that are of theoretical interest. The utility of doing so will be illustrated in later sections, but we establish the basic logic here. Suppose that prior to conducting the logistic analysis, we subtract a constant of 1 from the ideology scale. Whereas the original scale ranged from -3 to $+3$, the new scale ranges from -4 to $+2$, as each score is shifted down 1 unit. Here are the results for the logistic equation using this transformed score:

$$\text{logit}(\pi) = 1.042 + -1.712 \text{ gender} + -0.513 \text{ ideology}_t.$$

Note that the only parameter estimate affected by this transformation is the intercept, with the other coefficients being identical to those in the original analysis. The intercept is the predicted log odds when gender is 0 and when the transformed ideology value is 0. But a 0 on the transformed ideology variable represents a $+1$ on the original ideology variable. The intercept in this second analysis should equal the predicted log odds for females who have an ideology score of $+1$ in the original analysis. This is indeed the case. In the original equation

$$\text{logit}(\pi) = 1.555 + -1.712(0) + -0.513(1) = 1.042,$$

which is the same as the intercept in the second analysis. Why would one want to perform such transformations? Almost all computer packages report not only the parameter estimates for a logistic equation, but also the estimated standard errors and confidence intervals for a given parameter. Using transformations such as that above represents a simple if cumbersome way for calculating the confidence intervals for the odds for any given predictor profile. Simply transform each predictor by adding or subtracting a constant so that a score of 0 on the transformed variable represents the predictor value on the original scale that you are interested in. The exponent of the intercept term from the equation using the transformed predictors will then provide the predicted odds for that particular profile and the confidence intervals for the predicted odds will be those associated with the exponent of the intercept term. In the absence of transformations of this nature, the intercept term sometimes has limited interpretational value because it reflects the predicted log odds for the case where values of 0 on the predictors are nonexistent or outside of the range of the values being studied. We make use of the transformation strategy and variants of it in later chapters.

Definition of Interaction

There are many ways in which interaction effects have been conceptualized in the social sciences, but one of the most common frameworks uses the concepts of dependent variables, independent variables, and moderator variables. A dependent variable is an outcome variable that is thought to be determined or influenced by an independent variable. The independent variable is a presumed cause of the dependent variable. An interaction effect is said to exist when the effect of an independent variable on a dependent variable differs depending on the value of a third variable, commonly called a "moderator variable." For example, the effect of ideology on whether or not someone votes for a piece of legislation may differ for males and females. In this case, voting is the outcome or dependent variable, ideology is the independent variable, and gender is the moderator variable. As another example, the effect of social class on whether someone uses a health clinic may vary depending on ethnicity. In this case, use of a health clinic is the outcome or dependent variable, social class is the independent variable, and ethnicity is the moderator variable.

The "moderator approach" to interaction analysis requires that the theorist specify a moderator variable and what we call a *focal* independent variable, namely the independent variable whose effect on or relationship to the dependent variable is said to be moderated by the moderator variable. It is our experience that most formal research questions naturally lend themselves to the specification of one of the predictors as having "moderator" status and that such a designation is a useful heuristic for thinking about interactions. The designation of a moderator variable on conceptual grounds is often straightforward. For example, suppose one wants to determine whether a clinical treatment for depression is more effective for males than females. It is evident in this case that gender is the moderator variable and the presence versus absence of the treatment is the focal independent variable. On the other hand, there are situations where one theorist's moderator variable might be another theorist's focal independent variable and vice versa. For example, a consumer psychologist who studies product quality and product choice might be interested in the effect of product quality on product purchase decisions and how this is moderated by the pricing of products. In contrast, a marketing researcher using the same experimental paradigms as the consumer psychologist might be interested in the effect of product pricing on product purchase decisions and how this is moderated by product quality. In both cases, the designation of the moderator variable follows directly from the theoretical orientation of the researcher. Neither specification is better than the other and statistically the evalution of the presence of an interaction will not differ. The two designations simply represent different perspectives on the same phenomena.

The above is a general characterization of the nature of an interaction effect. We provide more precise statistical definitions in ensuing chapters. The moderator approach to interaction analysis is but one way of thinking about interaction parameters. Social scientists may choose to define interaction effects differently from this, with some preferring strictly statistical definitions and others preferring definitions tied to both a statistical model and a research design. Researchers also differ in how interactions are parameterized (Jaccard, 1998). Our approach is to define an interaction in general terms, using it to refer to cases where the relationship between two variables varies as a function of a third (moderator) variable (in the case of two-way interactions). Although we believe that this approach has widespread applicability and typifies the vast majority of applications in the social sciences, it does have limitations. Sometimes the assignment of one variable to moderator status and the other to focal independent variable status may seem too arbitrary, with the investigator wishing to entertain both variables in the respective roles of moderator variable and focal independent variable. There is nothing to prevent the researcher from characterizing the interaction from both perspectives, should this be the case. As will be shown in later chapters, the approach also tends to mask the fact that the same interaction parameter characterizes the effect of X on Y when Z is the moderator variable as well as the effect of Z on Y when X is the moderator. Despite these pedagogical shortcomings, we believe that most applied researchers (implicitly or explicitly) revert to a moderator framework when characterizing an interaction effect, probably because it is conceptually compelling to do so.

The most common approach to modeling interactions in logistic regression is to use product terms. Consider the following (noninteractive) model with two continuous predictors:

$$\text{logit}(\pi) = \alpha + \beta_1 X + \beta_2 Z.$$

To illustrate an interaction model, we conceptualize Z as the moderator variable and contend that in addition to the above effects there is an interaction effect such that the effect of X (the focal independent variable) on the outcome variable differs depending on the value of Z. One way of expressing this is to model β_1 (which reflects the effect of X on the outcome variable) as a linear function of Z:

$$\beta_1 = \alpha' + \beta_3 Z.$$

According to this formulation, for every 1 unit that Z changes, the value of β_1 is predicted to change by β_3 units. We now substitute the above expression for β_1 in the original equation, yielding

$$\text{logit}(\pi) = \alpha + (\alpha' + \beta_3 Z)X + \beta_2 Z.$$

Multiplying this out yields

$$\text{logit}(\pi) = \alpha + \alpha' X + \beta_3 XZ + \beta_2 Z,$$

and after assigning new labels to the coefficients and rearranging terms, we obtain an interaction model with a product term:

$$\text{logit}(\pi) = \alpha + \beta_1 X + \beta_2 Z + \beta_3 XZ.$$

Other conceptual specifications of interaction models lead to the same equation and other forms of interaction lead to different equations. Our point here is merely to show that including a product term in a model serves to introduce one type of interaction analysis (i.e., where the effect of the focal independent variable on the outcome variable is said to be a linear function of the moderator variable) and to draw attention to this frequently encountered equation. The remainder of this monograph develops examples that illustrate how to interpret the coefficients in such interactive logistic models. We do not dwell on evaluating overall model fit nor do we analyze residuals to ensure proper fitting models. This is not to say that such issues are unimportant. They are critical. However, our intent is to help readers make sense of the coefficients that result from interactive logistic models, and this will be the primary focus of our discussion.

Hierarchically Well-Formulated Models

Kleinbaum (1992) notes that interaction analysis in logistic regression typically uses hierarchically well formulated models. A hierarchically well-formulated (HWF) model is one in which all lower order components of the highest order interaction term are included in the model. For example, if interest is in a two-way interaction between X and Z, then a HWF model includes X, Z, and XZ as predictors. If interest is in a three-way interaction between Q, X, and Z, then a HWF model includes Q, X, Z, QX, QZ, XZ, and QXZ as predictors. For a qualitative predictor with dummy variables, D_1 and D_2, and a continuous predictor, Z, a HWF interaction model includes D_1, D_2, Z, $D_1 * Z$, and $D_2 * Z$. Most (but not all) applications of interaction analysis involve HWF models, and this is the assumed structure in the present monograph.

Given a HWF model, the typical strategy used to evaluate interactions is hierarchical analysis. Consider the three-way interaction model for continuous predictors, Q, X, and Z. The HWF model is

$$\text{logit}(\pi) = \alpha + \beta_1 Q + \beta_2 X + \beta_3 Z + \beta_4 QX$$
$$+ \beta_5 QZ + \beta_6 XZ + \beta_7 QXZ.$$

To test if the highest order interaction term, in this case QXZ, is nontrivial, one compares the fit of a model that includes the term(s) representing the interaction with a model that eliminates the term(s); i.e., it compares the above equation with

$$\text{logit}(\pi) = \alpha + \beta_1 Q + \beta_2 X + \beta_3 Z + \beta_4 QX + \beta_5 QZ + \beta_6 XZ.$$

If the difference in model fits is nontrivial, then this suggests that the interaction term is important and the equation is then interpreted using the methods discussed in later chapters. However, if the difference in the model fits is trivial, then the conclusion is that the interaction term is unnecessary and can be eliminated. For the present example, the revised model would then contain multiple two-way interactions. A two-way interaction term is evaluated by ensuring that the underlying model is HWF with respect to the interaction term of interest and then comparing model fit when the term is eliminated as opposed to when it is present in the model. Nuances in evaluating multiple interactions of the same order (e.g., multiple two-way interactions) are discussed in Chapter 5.

In the above example, the interaction between two variables was represented by a single product term; i.e., it was a single degree of freedom interaction. In such cases, the statistical significance of the interaction can be determined either by conducting a hierarchical test of changes in χ^2 values reflecting model fit or by examining the significance test of the logistic coefficient associated with the single product term. If the logistic coefficient for the product term is not statistically significant, this implies that the interaction effect is not statistically significant. In traditional ordinary least squares regression, the F test of the regression coefficient associated with a single degree of freedom interaction always will be identical to the hierarchical F test that compares the fit of models with and without the interaction term. In logistic regression, this may not be the case because investigators sometimes use one type of fit index for the hierarchical test (e.g., differences in χ^2 results based on likelihood ratio statistics) and an alternative criterion at the level of the coefficients (e.g., a Wald test). This represents an inconsistency in the investigator's logic, unless such a strategy is explicitly used to evaluate the robustness of the effect across different fit indices.

Sometimes omnibus interaction effects cannot be captured in a single product term, which is the case for interaction effects involving a qualitative variable with more than two levels. For example, the interaction effect between a qualitative variable represented by two dummy variables, D_1 and D_2, and a continuous variable, Z, is captured by the presence of two product terms in a HWF model: $D_1 Z$ and $D_2 Z$. This is because one must multiply all the variables representing one variable by all the variables representing the other variable to examine the interaction effect between the two. In such cases, the test of the omnibus interaction must rely on the hierarchical procedure because it is possible for an omnibus effect to be statistically significant but for the logistic coefficients associated with each product term to be statistically nonsignificant. The reason for this will be apparent in later chapters.

This monograph focuses on the interpretation of logistic coefficients and their estimated standard errors as typically provided in output from standard statistical software. Tests of statistical significance and confidence intervals for the coefficients are based on the classic Wald statistic, although readers are cautioned about the behavior of this test in small samples (see Agresti, 1996, p. 89; Hosmer & Lemeshow, 1989). Allison (1999b) discusses an alternative approach for generating significance tests and confidence intervals for coefficients in the traditional logistic model, called profile likelihood confidence intervals.

Product Term Analysis Versus Separate Logistic Regressions

Suppose one wanted to compare the effects of a continuous variable, X, on a dichotomous outcome variable, Y, for two different groups, males and females. It is not uncommon for researchers to do so by calculating separate logistic regression equations for males and females and then examining whether the logistic coefficient for X is "statistically significant" (i.e., has an associated p value less than 0.05) in both analyses. If the coefficient is statistically significant in one group but not in the other, then the conclusion is that X is more important for the one group than for the other. This logic is flawed because the researcher never performs a formal statistical test of the *difference* between the logistic coefficients for the two groups. For example, it is entirely possible for the coefficient in one group to have a p value of 0.051 associated with it and the coefficient for the other group to have a p value of 0.049. Even though one is statistically significant and the other is not, the coefficients are almost certain to be comparable in magnitude with trivial differences between them. Formal interaction analysis through product terms in a single equation is preferable because it provides a means of formally testing the difference between logistic coefficients.

2. INTERACTIONS BETWEEN QUALITATIVE PREDICTORS

This chapter considers the case in which the interaction effect of interest involves qualitative predictors. Such analyses require the use of dummy variables. We consider first the case of a two-way interaction and then the case of a three-way interaction. In the latter, we illustrate the inclusion of a covariate other than those involved in the interactive relationship.

Two-Way Interactions

A developmental psychologist was interested in studying sexual activity in young adolescents. She identified a sample of 7th-grade students and asked each adolescent whether or not he or she had engaged in sexual intercourse. This dichotomous variable was the outcome and was scored 1 if the adolescent had engaged in sex and 0 if he or she had not. The predictor variables were the gender of the respondent, D_M (scored $1 = $ male, $0 = $ female), and the employment status of the mother of the adolescent (full-time employed versus part-time employed versus unemployed). Table 1 presents the probabilities and the odds of engaging in sex for each cell of the 2×3 factorial design. Because employment status has three levels, it is represented using two dummy variables, D_{Full} (scored $1 = $ full-time employed, $0 = $ everyone else) and D_{Part} (scored $1 = $ part-time employed, $0 = $ everyone else). Females are the reference group for gender and unemployed is the reference group for employment status. To analyze the interaction between these variables, it is necessary to create product terms in which all the dummy variables for one of the variables are multiplied by all the dummy variables for the other variable. This yields two product terms, $D_M D_{Full}$ and $D_M D_{Part}$. These product terms are then entered into the logistic equation in conjunction with the other terms, D_M, D_{Full}, and D_{Part}.

As noted in Chapter 1, the omnibus interaction effect is tested using hierarchical logistic regression in which one determines whether the product terms significantly improve model fit over and above the case where no product terms are included in the model. This approach involves estimating a model χ^2 for each of the following

TABLE 1

Probabilities and Odds of Adolescent Engaging in Sex as a Function
of Gender and Employment Status of the Mother

	Full-Time Employed	Part-Time Employed	Unemployed
Probabilities			
Males	0.36	0.30	0.28
Females	0.32	0.13	0.26
Odds			
Males	0.5625	0.4286	0.3889
Females	0.4706	0.1494	0.3514

two equations,

$$\text{logit}(\pi) = \alpha + \beta_1 D_M + \beta_2 D_{\text{Full}} + \beta_3 D_{\text{Part}} \qquad [6]$$

$$\text{logit}(\pi) = \alpha + \beta_1 D_M + \beta_2 D_{\text{Full}} + \beta_3 D_{\text{Part}}$$
$$+ \beta_4 D_M D_{\text{Full}} + \beta_5 D_M D_{\text{Part}} \qquad [7]$$

and then subtracting the χ^2 for the "no interaction" model (Equation 6) from the χ^2 for the "interaction" model (Equation 7). The χ^2 for the no interaction model was 24.75 (df = 3) and for the interaction model it was 34.19 (df = 5). The difference in the χ^2 value is $34.19 - 24.75 = 9.44$, which is distributed as a χ^2 with degrees of freedom equal to the difference in their degrees of freedom, $5 - 3 = 2$. Consulting a table of critical χ^2 values for $\alpha = 0.05$ and df = 2, the χ^2 difference is statistically significant, implying a significant omnibus interaction effect. For more details of the logic of hierarchical testing in logistic regression, see Menard (1995).

Also of interest to investigators are the contrasts that are reflected in the coefficients of the interaction model. Table 2 presents the logistic coefficients, the exponents of each coefficient, and the 95% confidence intervals for the exponents. We focus first on the interpretation of the coefficients for the nonproduct terms.

As discussed in Chapter 1, the exponent of the coefficient for gender is an odds ratio that compares the odds of engaging in sex for the

TABLE 2
Logistic Coefficients for Qualitative Predictors: Two-Way Interaction

Predictor	Logistic Coefficient	Exponent of Coefficient	95% Lower Limit	95% Upper Limit	p Value
D_M	0.1015	1.1068	0.7116	1.7215	0.652
D_{Full}	0.2922	1.3394	0.8680	2.0666	0.187
D_{Part}	−0.8539	0.4257	0.2533	0.7155	0.001
$D_M * D_{Full}$	0.0769	1.0799	0.5894	1.9788	0.803
$D_M * D_{Part}$	0.9511	2.5886	1.3174	5.0864	0.005
Intercept	−1.0460	0.3514	0.2562	0.4819	

group scored 1 on the dummy variable (males) with the odds of engaging in sex for the reference group (females). A common mistake, however, is to interpret this coefficient as if it represents a nonconditioned main effect of gender (e.g., the effect of gender collapsing across or holding constant employment status). This is not the case. Because the dummy variable is part of the product terms in the equation, the coefficient is conditioned on the moderator variable being zero [see Jaccard, Turrisi, & Wan (1990) for elaboration of this concept]. Given the presence of the product terms, the exponent of the coefficient reflects the predicted odds ratio comparing males to females for the case in which the values on the other variable(s) involved in the product terms equal zero (i.e., for the case in which $D_{Full} = 0$ and $D_{Part} = 0$). Thus, the exponent of the coefficient for D_M is the predicted odds ratio for males to females but only for adolescents of unemployed mothers (because adolescents of unemployed mothers have scores of $D_{Full} = 0$ and $D_{Part} = 0$). In Table 1, note that the odds of engaging in sex for male adolescents of unemployed mothers is 0.3889 and the odds of engaging in sex for female adolescents of unemployed mothers is 0.3514. The ratio of these two odds, 0.3889/0.3514 = 1.1068, is the value of the exponent of the coefficient associated with gender. The 95% confidence interval for the exponent of the coefficient provides an appreciation for sampling error for the odds ratio. From Table 2, the 95% confidence interval was 0.7116 to 1.7215. Also, if the 95% confidence interval does not contain the value of 1.0, then the coefficient is said to be statistically significant (using an α level of 0.05) in traditional null hypothesis testing frameworks. In our example, the odds ratio does not differ significantly from 1.0 because the confidence interval contains the value of 1.0. It is entirely plausible that the odds of engaging in sex for sons of unemployed mothers equals the odds of engaging in sex for daughters of unemployed mothers in the population and the differences we observe in the sample are merely the result of sampling error.

A similar interpretation is imposed on the coefficients for D_{Full} and D_{Part}. The exponent of the coefficient for D_{Full} is 1.3394. This reflects an odds ratio comparing the predicted odds of engaging in sex by adolescents of full-time employed mothers to the predicted odds of engaging in sex by adolescents of unemployed mothers when gender = 0 (i.e., for females). From Table 1, the odds of engaging in sex for female adolescents of full-time employed mothers is 0.4706 and the odds of engaging in sex for female adolescents of unemployed mothers is 0.3514. The ratio of these two odds is 1.3394, which is the exponent of the coefficient for D_{Full}. The exponent of the coefficient for D_{Part} is 0.4257. This is an odds ratio comparing the predicted odds of engaging in sex for adolescents of part-time employed mothers to the predicted odds of engaging in sex for adolescents of unemployed mothers, when gender = 0 (i.e., for females). From Table 1, the odds of engaging in sex by female adolescents of part-time employed mothers is 0.1494 and the odds of engaging in sex by female adolescents of unemployed mothers is 0.3514. The ratio of these two odds is 0.4257, which is the exponent of the coefficient for D_{Part}. *For an interactive logistic model with two qualitative predictors, X and Z, and the relevant product terms for XZ (defined using dummy coding), the logistic coefficient for any dummy variable for X is conditioned to the reference group for Z. The exponent of the logistic coefficient for any dummy variable for X is the odds ratio that divides the predicted odds for the group scored 1 on the dummy variable for X by the predicted odds for the reference group on X, for the case where the dummy variables on Z equal zero.*

Next, let us examine the product term coefficients. Each of these coefficients represents a single degree of freedom interaction contrast. To conceptualize these contrasts, it is useful to specify the focal independent variable and the moderator variable. Suppose the investigator decides to treat gender as the focal independent variable and employment status of the mother as the moderator variable. Thus, the investigator is interested in how gender differences in the odds of engaging in sex differ as a function of the employment status of the mother. It will facilitate our discussion if we calculate the odds ratio comparing males to females for each level of the moderator variable. From Table 1, we have

OR for gender for full time mothers

$$= \frac{\text{odds for males}}{\text{odds for females}} = \frac{0.5625}{0.4706} = 1.1953$$

OR for gender for part time mothers

$$= \frac{\text{odds for males}}{\text{odds for females}} = \frac{0.4286}{0.1494} = 2.8688$$

OR for gender for unemployed mothers

$$= \frac{\text{odds for males}}{\text{odds for females}} = \frac{0.3889}{0.3514} = 1.1068.$$

If there is no interaction effect, then all of the odds ratios should be identical in value (except for sampling error). Different values for the three odds ratios imply that the effect of gender varies, depending on the employment status of the mother. Let us first compare the odds ratio for adolescents of full-time mothers (1.1953) to the odds ratio for adolescents of unemployed mothers (1.1068). We can form a ratio of the two odds ratios by dividing the odds ratio for gender for adolescents of full-time employed mothers by the odds ratio for gender for adolescents of unemployed mothers: 1.1953/1.1068 = 1.0799. If the two odds ratios are identical, then the ratio of the odds ratios should equal 1.0. As the two odds ratios diverge in value, the ratio of the odds ratios will diverge from 1.0. In this case, the odds ratio for gender for adolescents of full-time employed mothers is 1.0799 times larger than that for adolescents of unemployed mothers. Examine the exponent of the coefficient for $D_{M}D_{Full}$ in Table 2. Note that it equals 1.0799, the value of the ratio of the two odds ratios. The 95% confidence interval for this exponent provides a sense of sampling error for this interaction contrast, and the fact that the confidence interval includes the value of 1.0 suggests that the difference in odds ratios between the groups is not statistically significant. *For an interactive logistic model with two qualitative predictors, X and Z, and a product term, XZ, let X be the focal independent variable and let Z be the moderator variable. For the case of dummy coding, the exponent of the logistic coefficient for a product term is a ratio of predicted odds ratios. It focuses on the predicted odds for the group scored 1 on the dummy variable for X divided by the predicted odds for the reference group on X and divides this odds ratio when computed for the group scored 1 on the dummy variable for Z by the corresponding odds ratio for the reference group on Z.*

This logic also applies to the interpretation of the logistic coefficient for $D_M D_{Part}$. In this case, the exponent of the coefficient reflects the odds ratio for gender for adolescents of part-time mothers (2.8688) divided by the odds ratio for gender for adolescents of unemployed mothers (1.1068). This equals $2.8688/1.1068 = 2.5886$, which is the value of the exponent of the logistic coefficient for $D_M D_{Part}$. This contrast is statistically significant because the confidence interval does not include the value of 1.0.

Suppose that one is also interested in comparing the gender based odds ratio for adolescents of full-time employed mothers to that of part-time employed mothers. This contrast is not in the equation, yet it is also of theoretical interest. The easiest way to obtain the relevant statistics for this contrast is to simply respecify the dummy variables for the moderator variables by changing the group that is defined as the reference group. Then rerun the logistic regression analysis and examine the appropriate product term coefficient that corresponds to the contrast of interest. For example, if we redefined the dummy variables so that adolescents of part-time employed mothers is the reference group rather than adolescents of unemployed mothers, the resulting logistic equation will contain the contrast of interest. Note that when the dummy variables are respecified, the product terms also must be generated anew. The coefficients for the product terms will change in value because they now reflect different interaction contrasts. However, the omnibus hierarchical test of the interaction is unaffected by such rescoring.

For the sake of completeness, a comment should be made about the intercept term in the analysis. The exponent of the intercept term is the predicted odds when all predictors equal zero. In the present example, a zero on all predictors corresponds to the predictor profile of females with unemployed mothers (because for this group $D_M = 0$, $D_{Full} = 0$, and $D_{Part} = 0$ and the two product terms also equal 0). The exponent of the intercept is thus the predicted odds for this group (compare the value of the exponent of the intercept in Table 2 with the value of the odds for this group in Table 1 to verify this). The confidence interval for the exponent of the intercept provides information about the amount of sampling error associated with the estimate.

In sum, when product terms are included in a logistic equation with dummy variables, the coefficients for the "main effect" terms that are part of the product terms no longer represent main effects in the traditional sense. Rather, their exponents represent an odds ratio comparing the odds for the group scored 1 on the dummy variable with the odds for the reference group when the moderator variable(s) equal zero (i.e., for the moderator reference group). The exponent of the coefficient for a product term represents the ratio of two odds ratios.

The contrasts in Equation 7 were evaluated on a per contrast basis without regard to inflated error rates across the multiple contrasts that were performed. If there is concern about such error rates, one can apply a modified Bonferroni procedure to control the experimentwise error rates. In addition, simultaneous confidence intervals can be computed to evaluate the effects of sampling error in a multivariate sense. For more discussion of this topic, see Jaccard (1998) and Kirk (1995).

Three-Way Interactions

A researcher was interested in identifying factors that might improve the return of mail surveys. He sent a self administered survey to a sample of adults living in a community. Half of the individuals were provided a monetary incentive to return the survey ($10) while the other half were not. For half of the sample, the survey was relatively short, whereas for the other half of the sample the survey was relatively long. Finally, for half of the sample, the topic was a relatively important one whereas for the other half of the sample the topic was mundane. These three factors, monetary incentive, length of the survey, and importance of the topic, were varied in accord with a $2 \times 2 \times 2$ factorial design. To illustrate interpretational nuances when a covariate is included in the analysis, we assume the researcher had a measure of social class for each person who was sent a survey that was obtained from occupational information published in city directories. The social class measure ranged from 1 to 100 and the sample in question had a mean of 55 on this variable. The outcome measure was scored 1 if the respondent returned the survey and 0 if he or she did not.

To analyze a three-way interaction, it is helpful to first specify a focal independent variable and the moderator variables. However, for three-way interactions we need to impose further distinctions on the moderator variables because there are two of them. Suppose that the focal independent variable for this investigator was the monetary incentive and he wanted to determine whether the effects of the monetary incentive differed for mundane versus important topics. He hypothesized that the monetary incentive would have a greater effect when the survey was on a mundane topic than when it was on an important topic. When the topic is important, he reasoned, everyone will have an incentive to return the survey because the topic is compelling, so adding a monetary incentive on top of that will have trivial effects. By contrast, when the topic is mundane, individuals will be more likely to return the survey if they can benefit financially from doing so. The researcher further hypothesized that the qualifying nature of topic importance on the effects of monetary incentive would depend on the length of the survey. When the survey is long, people lose interest in completing it no matter how important the topic is or whether an incentive is provided. In such conditions, there will be no effect of a monetary incentive, and this will be true for both mundane and important topics. However, when the survey is short, the dynamics specified earlier will operate and there will be a two-way interaction such that the monetary incentive has a greater effect for mundane topics than for important ones. Topic importance is a *first-order moderator variable* because it is thought to directly moderate the impact of monetary incentive on return rates. Length of the survey is a *second-order moderator variable* because it moderates the impact of the first-order moderator on the relationship between the focal independent variable and the dependent variable. Again, it is not necessary to conceptualize three-way interactions in these terms. However, we have found this to be useful and have also found that when investigators describe the results of three-way interactions, they almost always adopt such an orientation to make sense of the complex relationships involved.

The researcher dummy coded each of the factors. For monetary incentive, D_M, a 1 was assigned to respondents who received an incentive and a 0 to respondents who did not. For topic importance, D_I, a 1 was assigned to respondents who received a survey on an important topic and a 0 was assigned to respondents who received a survey on a mundane topic. For survey length, D_L, a 1 was assigned to respondents who received a long survey and a 0 was assigned to respondents who received a short survey. Product terms were generated for the two-way interactions by multiplying the dummy variable for one factor by the dummy variable for the other factor.

This yielded three pairs of product terms, $D_M * D_I$, $D_M * D_L$, and $D_I * D_L$. A three-way product term also was generated: $D_M * D_I * D_L$. To make the intercept term more meaningful, the covariate, social class, was transformed by subtracting the sample mean (55.0) from each of the raw scores on social class prior to running the analysis. This transformation is called "mean centering". It does not affect any of the coefficients (or their estimated standard errors) for the other terms in the analysis, but it does affect the value of the intercept and the value of the predicted odds that we calculate later. The practice of mean centering quantitative covariates is common.

Table 3 presents the resulting logistic regression equation for the analysis. Because the three-way interaction has only a single degree of freedom, it is not necessary to perform a hierarchical test if one is interested in evaluating the omnibus three-way interaction effect. A statistically significant coefficient for the three-way interaction term implies a statistically significant omnibus effect given that the omnibus interaction has only a single degree of freedom. If an omnibus three-way interaction has more than a single degree of freedom, then a hierarchical test is required to evaluate it. As in the previous section, our focus will be on the exponents of coefficients.

The best way to appreciate the three-way interaction is to use the equation in Table 3 to calculate a predicted $\text{logit}(\pi)$ for each cell of the $2 \times 2 \times 2$ factorial design and then to convert these log odds to

TABLE 3

Logistic Coefficients for Qualitative Predictors: Three-Way Interaction

Predictor	Logistic Coefficient	Exponent of Coefficient	95% Lower Limit	95% Upper Limit	p Value
D_M	1.2905	3.6347	2.0141	6.5595	<0.001
D_I	1.2658	3.5458	1.9668	6.3925	<0.001
D_L	−0.1093	0.8965	0.4802	1.6736	0.732
$D_M * D_I$	−1.1939	0.3030	0.1336	0.6874	0.004
$D_M * D_L$	−1.2033	0.3002	0.1269	0.7100	0.006
$D_I * D_L$	−1.1420	0.3192	0.1353	0.7530	0.009
$D_I * D_M * D_L$	1.2187	3.3826	1.0227	11.1882	0.046
Class	0.0195	1.0197	1.008	1.0389	0.042
Intercept	−0.9140	0.4009	0.2592	0.6195	

TABLE 4

Predicted Odds and Odds Ratios for $2 \times 2 \times 2$ Factorial Design

	Short			Long	
	Mundane	*Important*		*Mundane*	*Important*
$10	1.4572	1.5659	$10	0.3922	0.4550
$0	0.4009	1.4216	$0	0.3594	0.4068
	1.4573/0.4009 = 3.6347	1.5659/1.4216 = 1.1015		0.3922/0.3594 = 1.0913	0.4550/0.4068 = 1.1185
	1.1015/3.6347 = 0.3030			1.1185/1.0913 = 1.0249	
		1.0249/0.3030 = 3.3826			

odds by calculating the exponent of each. In doing so, we set the value of the covariate, social class, equal to an arbitrary value, in this case 0. Recall that this score corresponds to the sample mean on the original social class measure. For the group that received no monetary incentive ($D_M = 0$) for a mundane survey ($D_I = 0$) that was short ($D_L = 0$), a value of 0 is entered for every predictor variable and the predicted log odds is -0.9140, which yields a predicted odds of 0.4009. This process is repeated for each of the eight groups defined by the factorial design and the predicted odds are tabled in the form of two 2×2 subtables in Table 4. When constructing such tables, it is helpful if the rows of the 2×2 subtable are the focal independent variable, the columns are the first-order moderator variable, and the variable that "splits up" the various 2×2 subtables is the second order moderator variable. Below each column of a 2×2 table, we compute an odds ratio that represents the predicted odds for the group scored 1 on the focal independent variable divided by the predicted odds for the reference group on the focal independent variable. Beneath each 2×2 subtable is the ratio of the odds ratio for the group scored 1 on the first order moderator variable divided by the odds ratio for the reference group on the first order moderator variable. These are the two-way interaction contrasts as defined in the previous section. If there is no three-way interaction effect, then the two-way interaction parameters should all be equal in value (except for sampling error) across the levels of the second order moderator variable. If they are different, then this implies that the nature of the two-way interaction depends on the value of the second order moderator. We can directly contrast the two two-way interaction parameters by taking the ratio of them. If the two-way interaction parameters are identical in value, then this ratio will equal 1.0. As the two-way interaction parameters diverge, the ratio of the two-way interaction parameters will diverge from 1.0. The bottom of Table 4 contains the ratio of the two-way interaction parameters for the group scored 1 on the second-order moderator divided by the two-way interaction parameter for the reference group on the second order moderator variable. It equals 3.3826.

Examine the exponent of the coefficient for the three-way product term in Table 3. Note that it equals 3.3826, the value of the ratio we just computed. *For an interactive logistic model with three qualitative predictors, X, Q, and Z, and the corresponding product terms between them, let X be the focal independent variable, let Q be the first order moderator variable, and let Z be the second-order moderator variable. For the case of dummy coding, the exponent of the logistic coefficient for a three-way product term is a ratio of two two-way interaction parameters. It focuses on the predicted odds for the group scored 1 on the dummy variable for X divided by the predicted odds for the reference group on X and divides this odds ratio for the group scored 1 on the dummy variable for Q by the corresponding odds ratio for the reference group on Q. This two-way interaction parameter is subjected to the three-way interaction contrast by dividing the parameter for the group scored 1 on Z by the parameter for the reference group on Z.* The 95% confidence interval for the exponent of this coefficient provides an appreciation for sampling error. If this interval contains the value of 1.0, then the three-way interaction contrast associated with the product term is not statistically significant.

The exponents of the coefficients for the two-way product terms each refer to a 2×2 subtable within the larger factorial design. However, because each of these terms is involved in a higher-order product term, they are conditioned on the second order moderator being zero. For example, examine the exponent of the product term associated with $D_M * D_I$ in Table 3. This equals 0.3030 and reflects the two-way interaction contrast between monetary incentive and topic importance when $D_L = 0$ (i.e., when the length is short). Verify this by examining the two-way interaction parameter for this contrast in Table 4. *For an interactive logistic model with three qualitative predictors, X, Q, and Z, and the corresponding product terms between them, for the case of dummy coding, the exponent of the logistic coefficient for a two-way* product term, *XZ*, is the two-way interaction parameter for *X* and *Z* when $Q = 0$.

Finally, the exponent of the coefficient for a "main effect" term in the equation reflects an odds ratio dividing the predicted odds for the group scored 1 on the dummy variable by the predicted odds for the reference group. Because the term is involved in product terms involving both moderator variables, it is conditioned on zero for both moderators and therefore represents an odds ratio for the reference group on both moderator variables. For example, the exponent of the coefficient associated with D_M is 3.6347, which is the odds ratio that divides the predicted odds of returning a survey for individuals with a monetary incentive by the predicted odds of returning a survey for individuals with no such incentive for the case of a short survey on a mundane topic. Verify this in Table 4. *For an interactive logistic model with three qualitative predictors, X, Q, and Z, and the corresponding product terms between them, for the case of dummy coding the exponent of the logistic coefficient for X is an odds ratio dividing the predicted odds for the group scored 1 on X by the predicted odds for the reference group on X considering only the reference groups on Q and Z.*

If confidence intervals are desired for a contrast not contained in the logistic equation, then the contrast can typically be isolated by redefining the reference group on one or both of the moderator variables and then rerunning the logistic regression so that the contrast is manifest in one of the coefficients in the equation.

The predicted odds in Table 4 were generated for the case where the covariate (social class) equaled the value of its sample mean. Although the value of the predicted odds would be different if they were generated at a different value of social class, the relations among them (i.e., the odds ratios, the ratios of the odds ratios, and the ratio of the ratio of the odds ratio) will be identical to those in Table 4. Interpretation of the exponent of the coefficient for the covariate follows standard protocol. In our example, the exponent for social class was 1.0197 (95% confidence interval = 1.0008 to 1.0389). This implies that for every 1 unit that social class increases, the predicted odds of returning a survey changes by a multiplicative factor of 1.0197, holding constant monetary incentive, topic importance, length of the survey, and all of the two-way interactions and the three-way interaction between these variables.

The above example considered the case in which the qualitative predictors have two levels. When a given predictor has three or more levels, then multiple dummy variables will be necessary to incorporate it into the analysis and multiple product terms will result. Each product term corresponds to a single degree of freedom contrast of either a conditioned main effect, a conditioned "two-way" interaction, or a three-way interaction parameter. The rules for which contrast is reflected by a product term coefficient follow directly from those rules specified above.

3. INTERACTIONS BETWEEN QUALITATIVE AND QUANTITATIVE/CONTINUOUS PREDICTORS

This chapter considers the case where the interaction effect of interest involves a mixture of categorical and quantitative/continuous predictors. The case of two-way interactions in which the qualitative variable is conceptualized as the moderator variable and the quantitative/continuous variable is the focal independent variable is considered first. The role of the two predictors is then reversed. Although the analyses use the identical logistic model and parameter estimates, the interpretation that the researcher imposes on them differs in terms of conceptual nuance. The chapter concludes by considering a three-way interaction involving two qualitative moderator variables and a quantitative/continuous focal independent variable.

Two-Way Interactions With a Qualitative Moderator Variable

An investigator was interested in the relationship between years of education and whether a community member would vote in a highly politicized special election in the community. He hypothesized that individuals with lower levels of education would be less likely to vote than individuals with higher levels of education. He also was interested in whether this relationship was comparable across different ethnic groups. The study that was conducted yielded information on voting behavior and education for each of three ethnic groups, blacks, Hispanics, and whites. In this case, whether someone voted is the outcome variable, education is the focal independent variable, and ethnicity is the moderator variable. Because ethnicity is a categorical variable, it is represented by two dummy variables, D_{black} and D_{Hispanic} with whites being treated as the reference group. Product terms are generated between each of these dummy variables and education and a logistic regression is performed using D_{black}, $D_{Hispanic}$, education, D_{black} * education and $D_{Hispanic}$ * education as predictors. Prior to forming the product terms, the researcher transformed the quantitative predictor. The modal number of years of education in the sample was 10, and this value was also the approximate median and mean amount of education. The investigator decided to subtract 10 from the original variable of education so that the zero point on the scale now corresponded to 10 years of education.

Table 5a presents the logistic coefficients, the exponents of the coefficients, and the 95% confidence interval for the exponents of the coefficients. The hierarchical test of the omnibus interaction effect showed a statistically significant ($p < 0.05$) effect. Our focus is on the interpretation of the coefficients in Table 5a. We consider only the coefficients for education and the product terms and defer consideration of the other coefficients to the next section, when the focal independent variable and moderator variables are reversed.

The logistic coefficient associated with education is 0.4556 and the exponent of the coefficient is 1.5772. Because education is part of the product terms, the coefficient associated with it does not represent a "main effect" but instead represents a conditional effect, i.e., the effect of education when the values on the moderator variable are zero. Thus, 1.5772 is the multiplicative factor by which the odds of voting changes for a 1-unit increase in education for whites (the reference group on the moderator variable). The confidence intervals for this parameter estimate provide a sense of sampling error (1.3003 to 1.9129). Because the confidence interval does not contain the value of 1.0, it is statistically significant. Examination of the exponent of the intercept reveals that the predicted odds of voting by whites with 10 years of education is 5.3026 (i.e., it is over 5 times more likely that whites with 10 years of education will vote than not vote). These predicted odds change by a factor of 1.5772 for every additional year of education. For example, the predicted odds of voting by whites with 11 years of education is $(5.3026)(1.5772) = 8.3633$ and for whites with 12 years of education it is $(8.3633)(1.5772) = 13.1906$. *For an interactive logistic model with a quantitative/continuous predictor, X, a qualitative predictor, Z, and a product term, XZ, for the case of dummy coding on Z, the exponent of the logistic coefficient for X is the multiplicative factor by which the predicted odds change given a 1-unit increase in X for the reference group on Z.*

TABLE 5

Logistic Coefficients for Qualitative and Quantitative Predictors:
Two-Way Interaction

Predictor	Logistic Coefficient	Exponent of Coefficient	95% Lower Limit	95% Upper Limit	p Value
a. Whites as Reference Group on Moderator Variable					
D_{black}	−0.8564	0.4247	0.1705	1.0575	0.066
$D_{Hispanic}$	−1.2082	0.2987	0.1082	0.8248	0.020
Education	0.4556	1.5772	1.3003	1.9129	<0.001
D_{black} * education	−0.1995	0.8191	0.6522	1.0288	0.086
$D_{Hispanic}$ * education	0.4584	1.5815	1.0216	2.4482	0.040
Intercept	1.6682	5.3026	2.4598	11.4309	
b. Hispanics as Reference Group on Moderator Variable					
D_{black}	0.3518	1.4216	0.6217	3.2506	0.404
D_{white}	1.2082	3.3475	1.2124	9.2426	0.020
Education	0.9140	2.4942	1.6853	3.6916	<0.001
D_{black} * education	−0.6579	0.5180	0.3436	0.7808	0.002
D_{white} * education	−0.4584	0.6323	0.4085	0.9789	0.040
Intercept	0.4600	1.5841	0.8151	3.0785	
c. Blacks as Reference Group on Moderator Variable					
$D_{Hispanic}$	−0.3518	0.7034	0.3076	1.6085	0.404
D_{white}	0.8564	2.3548	0.9456	5.8638	0.066
Education	0.2561	1.2919	1.1443	1.4585	<0.001
$D_{Hispanic}$ * education	0.6579	1.9307	1.2808	2.9103	0.002
D_{white} * education	0.1995	1.2208	0.9720	1.5333	0.086
Intercept	0.8118	2.2520	1.3764	3.7104	

As noted earlier, the investigator was interested in comparing the impact of education on voting behavior for each of the three ethnic groups. It will be instructive to derive the value of the multiplicative factor for education for each of the three ethnic groups. Although this can be accomplished through algebraic manipulation of the logistic equation in Table 5a (as described in Chapter 5), a simple method for obtaining the parameter estimate and the corresponding confidence interval for a given group is to redefine the dummy variables for the moderator variable so that a different group is the reference group. After doing so, regenerate the product terms and rerun the logistic analysis. In each case, the exponent of the logistic coefficient for education will yield the multiplicative factor for the reference group on the moderator variable, whoever that reference group may be. This strategy was employed in Table 5b using Hispanics as the reference group for ethnicity and in Table 5c using blacks as the reference group for ethnicity. From the three analyses in Table 5, we can characterize the multiplicative factor by which the predicted odds change for a 1-unit increase in education for each of the three ethnic groups:

	Multiplicative Factor	95% Lower Limit	95% Upper Limit
Blacks	1.2919	1.1443	1.4585
Hispanics	2.4942	1.6853	3.6916
Whites	1.5772	1.3003	1.9129

If education has the same effect for all three ethnic groups (i.e., if there is no interaction effect), then the multiplying factor should be the same in all three groups (except for sampling error). We can formally compare the multiplicative factor for blacks with that for whites by taking the ratio of the two multiplicative factors, $1.2919/1.5772 = 0.8191$. If the two multiplicative factors are equal, this ratio will equal 1. As the two multiplicative factors diverge, the value of this ratio will diverge from 1.0. In this case, the multiplicative factor for blacks is about 80% the magnitude of that for whites. Examine the exponent of the logistic coefficient for the product term for D_{black} * education in Table 5a. Note that it equals 0.8191, which is the ratio of the two multiplicative factors. The 95% confidence intervals (0.6522 to 1.0288) give a sense of the sampling error associated with this ratio. Because the confidence interval contains the value of 1.0, the differences in these multiplicative factors is deemed to be statistically nonsignificant. *For an interactive logistic model with a quantitative/continuous predictor, X, a qualitative predictor, Z, and a product term, XZ, for the case of dummy coding on Z, the exponent of the logistic coefficient for XZ is the ratio of the multiplicative factor by which the predicted odds change given a 1-unit increase in X for the group scored 1 on the dummy variable for Z divided by the corresponding multiplicative factor for the reference group on Z.* Any given logistic analysis reported in Table 5a to 5c isolates two of the three possible pairwise contrasts of multiplicative factors. The third can be obtained by redefining the reference group on the moderator variable and rerunning the analysis. Such rescoring affects the values of the coefficients associated with the product terms because they define different contrasts, but it does not affect the results of the hierarchical test of the omnibus interaction. Modified Bonferroni tests or simultaneous confidence intervals can be calculated to control for the fact that multiple contrasts are being performed (Jaccard, 1998).

Two-Way Interactions With a Quantitative Moderator Variable

Suppose that instead of the previous conceptual framework, the investigator was interested in comparing the voting behavior of the three ethnic groups and how these ethnic differences varied as a function of education. In this case, the outcome variable is voting behavior, the focal independent variable is ethnicity, and the moderator variable is education. This conceptual framework uses the same logistic analyses reported in Table 5a through 5c, but focuses on different coefficients and imposes a different theoretical interpretation on the coefficients. We now discuss the interpretation of the coefficients in Table 5 from this theoretical vantage point, focusing first on the dummy variables for ethnicity.

To clarify the meaning of the coefficients for the ethnicity dummy variables, we first specify the predicted odds of voting by blacks, whites, and Hispanics when education is at 10 years. The predicted odds for whites with 10 years of education is the exponent of the intercept in Table 5a, the predicted odds for Hispanics with 10 years of education is the exponent of the intercept in Table 5b, and the predicted odds for blacks with 10 years of education is the exponent of the intercept in Table 5c (recall that the education predictor was "centered about the value of 10"; hence the intercept isolates the odds of voting for the reference group when education is at 10 years):

	Predicted Odds of Voting	95% Lower Limit	95% Upper Limit
Blacks	2.2520	1.3764	3.7104
Hispanics	1.5841	0.8151	3.0785
Whites	5.3026	2.4598	11.4309

To explore ethnic differences in the odds of voting when education is at 10 years, we can compare the predicted odds for blacks with the predicted odds for whites by forming an odds ratio between the two,

$2.252/5.3026 = 0.4247$. Examine the exponent of the logistic coefficient associated with D_{black} in Table 5a. It equals 0.4247, the value of this odds ratio. *For an interactive logistic model with a qualitative predictor, X, a quantitative/continuous predictor, Z, and a product term, XZ, for the case of dummy coding of X, the exponent of the logistic coefficient for a dummy variable of X is the ratio of the predicted odds for the group scored 1 on the dummy variable divided by the predicted odds for the reference group on X, conditioned on Z being equal to 0.* The confidence interval for the exponent of the coefficient (0.1705 to 1.0575) provides an appreciation for sampling error and the fact that the interval contains the value of 1.0 means that the difference in odds between the two groups is not statistically significant.

We can use Table 5a through 5c to isolate the three pairwise odds ratios comparing blacks to whites (Table 5a), Hispanics to whites (Table 5a), and blacks to Hispanics (Table 5b) when education is at 10 years by examining the coefficients for appropriate dummy variables in the different analyses. The three comparisons are summarized as follows:

	Predicted Odds for Group Scored 1	Predicted Odds for Reference Group	Odds Ratio	95% Lower Limit	95% Upper Limit
Blacks versus whites	2.2520	5.3026	0.4247	0.1705	1.0575
Hispanics versus whites	1.5841	5.3026	0.2987	0.1082	0.8248
Blacks versus Hispanics	2.2520	1.5841	1.4216	0.6217	3.2506

If there is no interaction effect, then a given odds ratio should be of the same value when education is at 10 years as when education is equal to some other value, such as 11 years. For example, the odds ratio comparing blacks to whites is 0.4247 for 10 years of education and it should also be 0.4247 for 11 years of education. If this were not the case, then the impact of ethnicity on voting depends upon the level of education, which implies an interaction effect.

For expositional purposes, a second set of logistic analyses was performed comparable to those in Table 5, but in which education was transformed by subtracting 11 from the original education variable rather than 10. This defines the zero point for education at 11 years and permits us to reproduce the above table for the case where education is at 11 years rather than 10 years using the coefficients for the dummy variables. Here are the results, after recalculating the product terms using the transformed education variable, tabled:

	Predicted Odds for Group Scored 1	Predicted Odds for Reference Group	Odds Ratio	95% Lower Limit	95% Upper Limit
Blacks versus whites	2.9093	8.3637	0.3479	0.1199	1.0093
Hispanics versus whites	3.9511	8.3637	0.4724	0.1448	1.5417
Blacks versus Hispanics	2.9093	3.9511	0.7363	0.2911	1.8628

Focus first on the black versus white odds ratio. When education was at 10 years, the odds ratio was 0.4247. By contrast, when education is at 11 years, the odds ratio is 0.3479. If we take the ratio of these two results 0.3479/0.4247, we obtain 0.8191. When education increases by 1 unit (i.e., 1 year), the odds ratio comparing blacks to whites changes by a multiplicative factor of 0.8191. Now examine the exponent of the coefficient for the product term for D_{black} * education in Table 5a. It equals 0.8191, which is the factor by which the odds ratio changes given a 1-unit increase in the moderator variable, education. If education changed from 11 years to 12 years, then the odds ratio comparing blacks to whites would again change by this multiplicative factor: $(0.3479)(0.8191) = 0.2850$. *For an interactive logistic model with a qualitative predictor, X, a quantitative/continuous predictor, Z, and a product term, XZ, for the case of dummy coding on X, the exponent of the logistic coefficient for a product term indicates the multiplicative factor by which the odds ratio comparing the predicted odds for the group scored 1 on X and the predicted odds for the reference group on X changes given a 1-unit increase in Z.* The confidence interval for the exponent of a coefficient for a product term provides perspectives on sampling error and if the interval contains the value of 1.0, then the interaction contrast is statistically nonsignificant. In the present case, the confidence interval for the interaction contrast focused on blacks and whites contains the value of 1.0; hence the contrast is not statistically significant.

The same logic applies to the interpretation of the other product terms. In Table 5a, the exponent of the coefficient associated with $D_{Hispanic}$ * education is 1.5815. For every 1-unit increase in education, the odds ratio comparing the predicted odds for Hispanics with the predicted odds for whites changes by a multiplicative factor of 1.5815. In Table 5b, the exponent of the coefficient associated with $D_{black} * education$ is 0.5180. For every 1-unit increase in education, the odds ratio comparing the predicted odds for blacks with the predicted odds for Hispanics changes by a multiplicative factor of 0.5180. The confidence interval does not contain the value of 1.0, indicating that the result is statistically different.

Through the judicious use of transformations and choice of reference groups, it is possible to obtain parameter estimates and confidence intervals for a wide range of odds, odds ratios, multiplicative factors, ratios of odds ratios, and ratios of multiplicative factors. As before, simple additive transformations alter coefficients because they reflect different contrasts, but the omnibus hierarchical test of the interaction is unaffected. Covariates can be added to an equation to control for other variables and the same principles for interpreting coefficients in the presence of covariates described earlier apply.

Three-Way Interactions

A study was conducted in which an investigator examined whether parents attended a workshop offered at a local school on how to improve parent-adolescent communication about drug use. A parent in the sample was assigned a score of 1 if he or she attended the workshop and a score of 0 if he or she did not. A pamphlet describing the workshop was sent to all parents of students in the school, and they were invited to attend the workshop on a given evening of their choice. Earlier in the school year, a measure of how concerned parents were about their child using drugs was obtained. The measure ranged from 1 to 25, with higher scores indicating greater levels of concern. The investigator was interested in the relationship between stated concern about drug use and attendance behavior. She hypothesized that the effect of concern on attendance would be moderated by the employment status of the parent. If the parent was full-time employed, then it was hypothesized that concern for drug use would have less of an effect on workshop attendance. The rationale for this prediction was that full-time employed parents have more time constraints than non-full-time employed parents and even though they may be concerned about drug use, their more hectic time schedules make it more difficult for them to translate their concerns into behavior. This variable, called D_{ES}, was scored 1 if the parent was full-time employed; otherwise it was scored 0. As part of the study, the investigator also manipulated the number of choices the individual had as to the evening when he or she could attend the workshop. Half of the parents were told that the workshop was on a single evening and they were given no choice as to when to attend. The other half of the parents were given three evenings to choose from to attend the workshop. The investigator hypothesized that the moderating effects of employment status would only operate in the "no choice" condition as opposed to the "multiple choice" condition. The rationale for the prediction was that the flexibility provided in the scheduling of multiple workshops from which to choose would negate the constraining effects of employment status. The choice variable, called D_C, was scored 1 if the parent was given multiple choices and 0 if the parent was given no choices.

In this study, attendance at the workshop is the outcome variable, parental concern for drug use is the focal independent variable, employment status is the first-order moderator variable, and the number of workshop choices is the second order moderator variable. The researcher decided to mean center the continuous predictor, concern for drug use, to facilitate interpretation of the intercept term. The transformed concern scores were then used to form product terms with D_{ES} and D_C. A measure of social class was included as a covariate, and it also was mean centered.

It will be easier to convey the meaning of the product term coefficients if we first isolate the logistic coefficient for the focal independent variable for each of the four groups. Although this can be done algebraically from a single logistic analysis, it is simpler to isolate these coefficients and their confidence intervals by calculating four different logistic analyses, each time redefining the reference groups on the two dummy variables so that each of the four groups within the 2×2 design takes a turn as the reference group across the two dummy variables. This has been done in Table 6a through 6d. Using the principles from previous sections, the logistic coefficient for concern in any given analysis is conditioned on the moderators being zero and reflects the impact of concern on attendance behavior when $D_{ES} = 0$ and when $D_C = 0$ (holding social class constant). It thus focuses on the effect of concern for the reference groups on employment status and whether choices were given. The coefficients for the four groups and the 95% confidence intervals for the exponents of the coefficients are:

	Logistic Coefficient	Exponent of Coefficient	95% Lower Limit	95% Upper Limit
Choice, full-time (Table 6a)	0.1831	1.2010	1.1351	1.2707
Choice, not full-time (Table 6b)	0.1242	1.1323	1.0754	1.1921
No Choice, full-time (Table 6c)	0.0721	1.0747	1.0141	1.1390
No Choice, not full-time (Table 6d)	0.1520	1.1642	1.1058	1.2256

Let us first obtain an index of the differential impact of concern for full-time versus not full-time employed parents under the condition of

TABLE 6
Logistic Coefficients for Qualitative and Quantitative Predictors: Three-Way Interaction

Predictor	Logistic Coefficient	Exponent of Coefficient	95% Lower Limit	95% Upper Limit	p Value
a. Choice, Full-Time Group (D_C is 1 = no choice, 0 = choice; D_{ES} is 1 = not full-time, 0 = full-time)					
D_{ES}	0.2491	1.2829	1.0280	1.6009	0.028
D_C	−0.2788	0.7567	0.5990	0.9560	0.019
Concern	0.1831	1.2010	1.1351	1.2707	<0.001
Social class	0.0516	1.0529	1.0133	1.0941	0.008
$D_{ES} * D_C$	0.1270	1.1354	0.8249	1.5630	0.436
$D_{ES} *$ concern	−0.0589	0.9428	0.8735	1.0175	0.130
$D_C *$ concern	−0.1111	0.8949	0.8254	0.9702	0.007
$D_{ES} * D_C *$ concern	0.1389	1.1490	1.0306	1.2810	0.012
Intercept	−0.9839	0.3739	0.3180	0.4395	
b. Choice, Not Full-Time Group (D_C is 1 = no choice, 0 = choice; D_{ES} is 1 = full-time, 0 = not full-time)					
D_{ES}	−0.2491	0.7795	0.6246	0.9728	0.028
D_C	−0.1517	0.8592	0.6910	1.0684	0.172
Concern	0.1242	1.1323	1.0754	1.1921	<0.001
Social class	0.0516	1.0529	1.0133	1.0941	0.008
$D_{ES} * D_C$	−0.1270	0.8807	0.6398	1.2123	0.436
$D_{ES} *$ concern	0.0589	1.0607	0.9828	1.1448	0.130
$D_C *$ concern	0.0278	1.0282	0.9560	1.1058	0.454
$D_{ES} * D_C *$ concern	−0.1389	0.8703	0.7806	0.9703	0.012
Intercept	−0.7348	0.4796	0.4123	0.5579	

TABLE 6 Continued

Predictor	Logistic Coefficient	Exponent of Coefficient	95% Lower Limit	95% Upper Limit	p Value
c. No Choice, Full Time Group (D_C is 1 = choice, 0 = no choice; D_{ES} is 1 = not full-time, 0 = full time)					
D_{ES}	0.3761	1.4566	1.1569	1.8340	0.001
D_C	0.2788	1.3215	1.0460	1.6695	0.019
Concern	0.0721	1.0747	1.0141	1.1390	0.015
Social class	0.0516	1.0529	1.0133	1.0941	0.008
$D_{ES} * D_C$	−0.1270	0.8807	0.6398	1.2123	0.436
$D_{ES} *$ concern	0.0799	1.0832	1.0024	1.1706	0.043
$D_C *$ concern	0.1111	1.1175	1.0307	1.2116	0.007
$D_{ES} * D_C *$ concern	−0.1389	0.8703	0.7806	0.9703	0.012
Intercept	−1.2627	0.2829	0.2389	0.3350	
d. No Choice, Not Full-Time Group (D_C is 1 = choice, 0 = no choice; D_{ES} is 1 = full-time, 0 = not full-time)					
D_{ES}	−0.3761	0.6865	0.5453	0.8644	0.001
D_C	0.1517	1.1638	0.9360	1.4472	0.172
Concern	0.1520	1.1642	1.1058	1.2256	<0.001
Social class	0.0516	1.0529	1.0133	1.0941	0.008
$D_{ES} * D_C$	0.1270	1.1354	0.8249	1.5630	0.436
$D_{ES} *$ concern	−0.0799	0.9232	0.8543	0.9976	0.043
$D_C *$ concern	−0.0278	0.9726	0.9043	1.0460	0.454
$D_{ES} * D_C *$ concern	0.1389	1.1490	1.0306	1.2810	0.012
Intercept	−0.8866	0.4121	0.3523	0.4819	

having a choice of programs. The multiplying factor for concern for full-time employed parents is 1.2010 and for not full-time employed parents it is 1.1323. The ratio of these two multiplying factors is $1.2010/1.1323 = 1.0607$. The greater the discrepancy between the two multiplying factors, the more this ratio will depart from 1.0. This ratio is essentially a two-way interaction contrast (between concern and employment status) when the second-order moderator variable is held constant at the value of "choice."

We can calculate the same index for parents who were not given a choice. The multiplying factor for concern for full-time employed parents is 1.0747 and for not full-time employed parents it is 1.1642. The ratio of these two multiplying factors is $1.0747/1.1642 = 0.9232$.

We can now compare these two two-way interactions to gain perspectives on the three-way interaction. Specifically we form a ratio of the two two-way ratios, 1.0607/0.9232 = 1.1490. If there is no three-way interaction effect, then this index will equal 1.0 (except for sampling error). We could use any of the tables to illustrate our next point, but we will focus on Table 6d which scores D_C as 1 = "choice" and 0 = "no choice" and D_{ES} as 1 = "full-time" and 0 = "not full-time." Examine the exponent of the coefficient for the three-way product term in Table 6d. Note that it equals 1.1490, the value of the ratio of the ratio of multiplying factors. *For an interactive logistic model with a quantitative/continuous predictor, X, two qualitative predictors, Q and Z, and the corresponding product terms between them, let X be the focal independent variable, let Q be the first-order moderator variable, and let Z be the second-order moderator variable. For dummy coding on the qualitative predictors, the exponent of the logistic coefficient for the "three-way" product term is a ratio of the ratio of multiplying factors for X. The ratio focuses on the multiplying factor for X for the group scored 1 on the dummy variable for Q divided by the corresponding multiplying factor for the reference group on Q. This ratio for the group scored 1 on the dummy variable for Z is divided by the corresponding ratio for the reference group on Z.* The confidence intervals for this coefficient provide a sense of sampling error for the three-way interaction parameter estimate.

For the analysis in Table 6d, examine the exponent of the logistic coefficient for the product term D_{ES} * concern. Note that it equals the two-way interaction parameter that was calculated above for parents who were the reference group on the second-order moderator variable (0.9232), in this case, parents who were not given a choice. *For an interactive logistic model with a quantitative/continuous predictor, X, two qualitative predictors Q and Z, and the corresponding product terms between them, the exponent of the logistic coefficient for the XQ product term will equal the two-way interaction parameter for XQ when Z = 0.* The confidence intervals for this coefficient provide a sense of sampling error for this two-way interaction parameter estimate.

Examination of Tables 6a through 6d shows that the values of the coefficients for the product terms change as different reference groups are defined because the reference group that is a part of the contrast isolated by the product term is being changed. This also changes the group that defines the conditional "zero" for the "main effect" terms. However, the rules stated above dictate the interpretation of a given coefficient, and the results of all the analyses are entirely consistent with one another.

4. INTERACTIONS BETWEEN QUANTITATIVE/CONTINUOUS PREDICTORS

This chapter considers the case in which the interaction effect of interest is located in the moderating effects of a quantitative/continuous predictor on the effects of another quantitative/ continuous predictor. We consider first the case of two-way interactions and then the case of three-way interactions.

Two-Way Interactions

An investigator studied factors having an impact on whether people in a high-risk population voluntarily take a test for the acquired immunodeficiency syndrome virus, human immuno deficiency virus (HIV) when it is offered to them for free. The researcher measured the individuals' perceived risk of getting HIV and the perceived severity of how devastating the consequences would be if HIV were contracted. Both constructs were measured on scales from 0 to 30 with higher scores indicating greater perceived risk and greater perceived severity, respectively. The researcher hypothesized that the impact of perceived risk would be greater as the perceived severity of the consequences of contracting the virus increased. In this case, test-taking behavior is the outcome variable, perceived risk is the focal independent variable, and perceived severity is the moderator variable. A logistic regression analysis was performed on test-taking behavior (1 = takes a test, 0 = does not take a test) using perceived risk, perceived severity, and a product term that multiplies the two variables by one another as predictor variables. Before conducting the analysis, the investigator decided to mean center the two predictors. Perceived risk had a mean of 14.792 and perceived severity had a mean of 13.108. The value of 14.792 was subtracted from each perceived risk score and the value of 13.108 was subtracted from each perceived severity score. A product term was then formed from these transformed scores. Table 7a presents the results of the analysis.

The exponent of the intercept is the predicted odds of taking an HIV test when both perceived risk and perceived severity equal their sample mean. In this case, the predicted probability of taking an HIV test is 1.2866 times larger than the predicted probability of not taking the test. The exponent of the coefficient for the focal independent variable, perceived risk, is 1.2338. Because perceived risk is part of the

TABLE 7
Logistic Coefficients for Two Quantitative Predictors:
Two-Way Interaction

Predictor	Logistic Coefficient	Exponent of Coefficient	95% Lower Limit	95% Upper Limit	p Value
(a) Analysis Using Mean Centered Predictors					
Risk	0.2101	1.2338	1.1609	1.3114	<0.001
Severity	0.3592	1.4322	1.2709	1.6139	<0.001
Risk * Severity	0.0559	1.0575	1.0265	1.0894	<0.001
Intercept	0.2520	1.2866	1.0239	1.6166	
(b) Analysis Using Mean Centered Perceived Risk and Perceived Severity Centered at 14.108					
Risk	0.2660	1.3047	1.2066	1.4108	<0.001
Severity	0.3592	1.4322	1.2709	1.6139	<0.001
Risk * Severity	0.0559	1.0575	1.0265	1.0894	<0.001
Intercept	0.6111	1.8425	1.3943	2.4347	

product term, this is a conditioned coefficient, so it reflects the effect of perceived risk when perceived severity equals zero (or in this case, when perceived severity equals its sample mean). When perceived severity is at its sample mean, a 1 unit increase in perceived risk results in the predicted odds of taking an HIV test changing by a multiplicative factor of 1.2338. For example, the predicted odds of taking an HIV test when perceived risk and perceived severity equal their sample means is 1.2866 (the exponent of the intercept). If perceived risk increases by 1 unit (from its mean of 14.792 to 15.792), then the predicted odds of taking an HIV test is $(1.2866)(1.2338) = 1.5874$ (holding perceived severity constant at the value of its sample mean). *For an interactive logistic model with two quantitative predictors, X and Z, and a product term, XZ, the exponent of the logistic coefficient for X equals a multiplicative factor by which the predicted odds change given a 1-unit increase in X when Z = 0.*

To illustrate the meaning of the coefficient for the product term, we redo the analysis but instead of subtracting a constant of 13.108 from perceived severity (its sample mean value), we subtract a value of 14.108 (i.e., we make the zero point on perceived severity be 1 unit higher than in the previous analysis). Table 7b presents the results of this analysis. The exponent of the logistic coefficient for

perceived risk is now 1.3047. From the previous analysis, when perceived severity equaled 13.108 the exponent of the coefficient was
1.2338. When perceived severity increases by 1 unit (to 14.108), the
exponent of the perceived risk coefficient is 1.3047. If we take the
ratio of these two results, we find that a 1 unit change in perceived
severity causes the impact of perceived risk (as indexed by its multiplicative factor) to increase by a factor of 1.3047/1.2338 = 1.0575.
Examine the exponent of the product term in Table 7a. It equals
1.0575. The exponent of this coefficient tells us by what factor the
multiplying factor of perceived risk changes given a 1 unit increase
in perceived severity. If we increased perceived severity by another
unit to 15.108, then the multiplying factor for perceived risk would be
(1.3047)(1.0575) = 1.3797. The confidence interval for the exponent
of the coefficient of the product term provides an appreciation for
sampling error and if the interval contains the value of 1.0, then the
interaction effect is not significant. *For an interactive logistic model
with two quantitative/continuous predictors, X and Z, and a product
term, XZ, the exponent of the logistic coefficient for the product term is
the multiplicative factor by which the multiplicative factor of X changes
given a 1-unit increase in Z.* Note that the transformation we performed does not affect the value of the product term coefficient; i.e.,
it is invariant across simple additive transformations.

Three-Way Interactions

A social worker conducted a study of suicide contemplation in
which the outcome variable was a self-report by a sample of patients
of whether he or she had contemplated suicide during the past
6 months (scored 1 = yes, 0 = no). The focal independent variable was how much stress the individual had experienced during
the past 6 months, which was measured on a 40-point scale, with
higher scores indicating greater levels of stress felt. The investigator
hypothesized that higher levels of stress would be associated with a
higher likelihood of suicide contemplation. The effect of stress on
suicide contemplation was predicted to be moderated by the strength
of the individual's social network. A weak support network, it was
hypothesized, would exacerbate the effects of stress on suicide contemplation. A measure of lack of support was obtained using a social
support scale, with scores ranging from 0 to 40. Higher scores indicated a weaker support network. Weakness of the support network is

a first-order moderator variable. The researcher further hypothesized that the effects of a weak support network would differ depending on how depressed the individual was. The less depressed the individual, the less that a weak support network would exacerbate the effects of stress on suicide contemplation. Depression was measured on a scale ranging from 0 to 50, with higher scores indicating greater levels of depression. Depression is a second-order moderator variable in the researcher's conceptual framework. The researcher mean centered each of the predictors and then calculated all possible two-way product terms and the three-way product term. Table 8 presents the results of the logistic regression.

Based on the principles presented in the previous section, the exponent of the coefficient for stress represents the multiplying factor by which the odds of suicide contemplation are predicted to change given a 1-unit increase in stress when social support and depression equal zero (i.e., when social support and depression are average, based on the mean centering). The multiplying factor is 1.1115 (95% confidence interval = 1.0911 to 1.1323). The exponent of the coefficient for the stress * support term reflects the two-way interaction contrast between stress and social support when depression equals zero (i.e., when depression is average). The exponent of this coefficient was 1.0289 (95% confidence interval = 1.0241 to 1.0337). This is the factor by which the multiplying factor for stress changes given a 1-unit increase in the measure of weakness of support when depression is average. For every 1 unit weaker that the

TABLE 8
Logistic Coefficients for Three Quantitative Predictors:
Three-Way Interaction

Predictor	Logistic Coefficient	Exponent of Coefficient	95% Lower Limit	95% Upper Limit	p Value
Stress	0.1057	1.1115	1.0911	1.1323	<0.001
Support	0.1046	1.1102	1.0891	1.1318	<0.001
Depression	0.1212	1.1288	1.1077	1.1504	<0.001
Stress * Support	0.0285	1.0289	1.0241	1.0337	<0.001
Stress * Depression	−0.0006	0.9994	0.9952	1.0037	0.786
Support * Depression	0.0010	1.0010	0.9966	1.0055	0.648
Three-way	0.0130	1.0131	1.0118	1.0144	<0.001
intercept	−1.4765	0.2284	0.2099	0.2502	

support gets, the effect of stress on the odds of suicide contemplation changes by a factor of 1.0289 (holding depression constant at its sample mean). Suppose we recalculate the exponent for the coefficient of the stress * support product term for the case in which depression is 1 unit above its sample mean rather than at its sample mean. This can be accomplished by centering depression at 21 instead of at 20 (which was the value of the original sample mean), recalculating the product terms, and rerunning the logistic analysis. The exponent of the coefficient for the stress * support product term in this analysis is 1.0424. We can index the change in the two-way interaction parameter that occurred from the previous analysis by dividing the value of the parameter in the first analysis by the value of the parameter in the second analysis. This yields 1.0424/1.0289 = 1.0131. If the two two-way interactions are identical in value, then this ratio will equal 1.0. Examine the exponent of the coefficient for the three-way product term in Table 8. It equals 1.0131, the value of the ratio of the two two-way interaction parameters. *For an interactive logistic model with three quantitative/continuous predictors, X, Q, and Z, and the various product terms between them, let X be the focal independent variable, let Q be the first-order moderator variable, and let Z be the second-order moderator variable. The exponent of the logistic coefficient for the three-way product term is the multiplicative factor by which the two-way interaction parameter for X and Q changes given a 1-unit increase in Z.* If we rerun the logistic regression centering depression 2 units above its sample mean, then the coefficient for stress * support would be (1.0424)(1.0131) = 1.0561.

5. MULTICATEGORY MODELS

The examples considered thus far focus on the case of a dichotomous outcome variable. Logit based models also have been developed for the analysis of outcomes with more than two categories. This chapter illustrates the interpretation of product terms for selected models of this nature. As in previous chapters, we assume that the reader is familiar with the fundamentals of multicategory logit models and concentrate on the interpretation of coefficients rather than on the evaluation of model fit.

Ordinal Regression Models

Ordinal regression models focus on outcome variables that are ordinal in character. Of the many types of models, one of the more popular is adjacent category ordinal regression (Agresti, 1996). Consider the case of an outcome variable with four ordered categories, 1 through 4, that is predicted from two continuous variables, X and Z. It is possible to calculate three logistic regressions comparing adjacent categories on the outcome variable. A logistic regression can be conducted focusing only on individuals with scores of 1 or 2 on the outcome variable that predicts this newly defined dichotomous outcome from X and Z. Similarly, an analysis can be performed focusing only on individuals with scores of 2 or 3 on the outcome variable and then again focusing only on individuals with scores of 3 and 4. Essentially, a set of pairwise logistic regressions are conducted where the defined pairs are based on adjacent categories of the outcome variable. The parameter estimates for the three equations are derived using a simultaneous solution (rather than a piecemeal one) and constraints are imposed on the coefficients (but not the intercepts) across the three equations. Specifically, the constraint that the coefficients for X must be equal across the three equations is imposed as is the constraint that the coefficients for Z must be equal across the three equations. This constrained model, which is more parsimonious then the unconstrained model because there is a single coefficient value for each predictor across the three equations, is commonly applied in adjacent category logit models [although unconstrained models also can be estimated as can models with constraints different from those specified above; see Agresti (1996)]. A product term can be added to the models to reflect an interaction between X and Z. The interpretation of the constrained coefficients associated with X, Z, and XZ follows the same basic principles as those discussed in this monograph, because in the final analysis, the multiple equations represent the analysis of log odds for adjacent categories using a logistic based model.

We illustrate the approach for a five-point outcome variable in which immigrants to the United States provide a self-rating of how conservative or liberal they are, where $1 =$ very conservative, $2 =$ somewhat conservative, $3 =$ moderate, $4 =$ somewhat liberal, and $5 =$ very liberal. The focal independent variable is the gender of the individual, scored as 1 = female and 0 = male. The investigator is interested in whether the effect of gender on political ideology varies as a function of the amount of time that the immigrant has lived in the United States (measured in years but with fractions to reflect the number of months and days lived in the United States as well). Among nonimmigrants in the United States, women tend to be more liberal than men. The researcher hypothesized that the political ideology of new immigrants would be similar for men and women, but with increased residency, the immigrants would become assimilated to U.S. culture, resulting in the emergence of the traditional gender difference. The analyst decided to treat the outcome variable as ordinal in character, the focal independent variable (gender) as categorical, and the moderator variable (length of residency) as continuous. Length of residency was mean centered prior to analysis.

The data were analyzed using a computer program called Goldminer, which is available in SPSS. The intercept terms were allowed to vary, but the coefficients for the three predictor variables (gender, residency, and gender * residency) were constrained to be equal across the four adjacent category logistic regressions. The analysis was undertaken, comparing categories 2 to 1, categories 3 to 2, categories 4 to 3, and categories 5 to 4. The logistic coefficients for gender, residency, and the product term were 0.44, 0.00, and −0.03. The exponents of the coefficients were 1.55, 1.00, and 0.97, respectively. The exponent of the coefficient for gender (1.55) reflects the effect of gender on political ideology when the length of residency is equal to its sample mean. In this case, the estimated odds that a female's ideology classification is in category $j + 1$ instead of category j are 1.55 times higher than the corresponding estimated odds for males when residency is at the value of its sample mean. The exponent of the product term indicates the multiplying factor by which this odds ratio is predicted to change given a 1-unit increase in the residency variable. For each additional year of residency, the gender-based odds ratio changes by a multiplying factor of 0.97 (using the logic developed in Chapter 3 for the case of a qualitative focal independent variable and a continuous moderator variable). The coefficient for the product term was not statistically significant ($p > 0.05$) and the 95% confidence interval for the exponent of the coefficient included the value of 1.0 (95% confidence interval = 0.91 to 1.02). The intercept for each of the four equations yielded by the analysis is the predicted odds of being in a given category relative to the category below it when all predictors equal zero (i.e., when gender and the mean centered years of residency both equal zero).

Given a trivial and nonsignificant interaction effect, it makes sense to reestimate the equation with the product term eliminated so that one can examine the "main effects" of gender and years of residency rather than the conditioned effects that emerge with the inclusion of the product term. The analysis that omitted the product term yielded a logistic coefficient for gender of 0.44 and a coefficient for years of residence of -0.02. Only the coefficient for gender was statistically significant ($p < 0.05$). The exponent of the coefficient for gender was 1.54 and the 95% confidence interval was 1.38 to 1.74. Thus, holding the number of years of residence constant, the predicted odds that a female's ideology classification is in category $j + 1$ instead of category j is 1.54 times higher than the corresponding predicted odds for males. For example, the predicted odds that a female is "very liberal" instead of "somewhat liberal" is 1.54 times higher than the corresponding predicted odds for males. Similarly, the predicted odds that a female is "somewhat liberal" instead of "moderate" is 1.54 times higher than the corresponding predicted odds for males. As a general rule for this type of model, for any two values, a and b, on the outcome variable and where $a > b$, the predicted odds ratio that an individual is in category a relative to category b will equal the exponent of the coefficient for a given predictor variable raised to the value of $a - b$. For example, the predicted odds ratio for gender when category 5 ("very liberal") is compared with category 1 ("very conservative") is $1.54^{(5-1)} = 5.7$. The predicted odds that a female identifies herself as "very liberal" as opposed to "very conservative" is 5.7 times greater than the predicted odds that a male identifies himself as "very liberal" as opposed to "very conservative."

There are a variety of ordinal regression models, many of which do not rely on logit functions. Model fit indices permit one to examine the plausibility of equation constraints as well as other model assumptions. Such evaluation is crucial before the coefficients yielded by the model are interpreted. For excellent discussions of a variety of approaches to ordinal regression, see Agresti (1996), Long (1997), and Magidson (1998).

Multicategory Nominal Variables

When the outcome variable is categorical and has more than two levels, analysis is often enacted in the context of the multinomial distribution. Consider the case where there are three categories on the outcome variable (A, B, and C) and two continuous predictors, X and Z. It is possible to conduct three "logistic regressions" based on all possible pairs of categories defined by the outcome variable; i.e., we can predict A versus B from X and Z, A versus C from X and Z, and B versus C from X and Z. When considered as a collective, the three equations are not independent and one would expect certain regularities across the equations. For example, knowing how X and Z affect the log odds of A versus B, as well as how X and Z affect the log odds of A versus C, necessarily tells us information about how X and Z affect the log odds of B versus C [see Long (1997) for elaboration]. The multinomial model yields simultaneous estimates for selected pairwise equations taking such dependencies into account. The "pairs" of categories estimated in the multinomial model can take many forms. The equations that result from most of these models are similar to those reported in this monograph because they characterize a binary outcome comparison in terms of log odds. The same interpretational framework for coefficients presented in this monograph can be applied to these models as well.[2]

A common multicategory model is called the *baseline-category model*. Given k levels of an outcome variable, one of the levels is declared by the researcher as the "baseline" or reference group. The analysis involves the estimation of $k - 1$ equations where each equation represents a logistic model comparing each of the other levels of the outcome variable with the reference group. For example, an outcome variable might be the political party with which someone affiliates, with four categories Democratic, Republican, Reform, and Independent. The outcome is predicted from two variables, X and Z. The baseline group might be defined by the researcher as the Independents. Three equations (i.e., $4-1$) are generated, one predicting Democrats versus Independents from X and Z, one predicting Republicans versus Independents from X and Z, and a third predicting Reformists versus Independents from X and Z. The solution for the coefficients in the three equations is based on a simultaneous algorithm. Unlike in ordinal regression, the focus is not restricted to "adjacent categories," and no constraints are imposed on the coefficients across equations (although constraints can be introduced if it is theoretically desirable to do so). The coefficients from the three equations can then be used to derive the values of the coefficients for equations comparing any two pairs of categories of the outcome variable [e.g., Democrats versus Republicans; see Agresti (1996)].

To illustrate, a developmental psychologist studied three types of attachment patterns that young children show with respect to their caretaker. The first type was secure attachment in which the child has a healthy, positive attachment to the caretaker. The second type was clinging, in which the child clings excessively to the caretaker and shows patterns of unhealthy dependency. The third type was avoidance, in which the child maintains distance from the caretaker and shows aloofness to him or her. The type of attachment pattern exhibited by a child was predicted from two variables. The first was a dichotomous variable that indicated whether the child's physical environment in the home is positive (scored 1) or negative (scored 0). The second was a continuous measure of how affectionate the mother is toward the child, with higher scores indicating greater degrees of affection (on a 0 to 10 scale). The researcher hypothesized that higher levels of affection would lead to higher odds of secure attachment relative to each of the other two forms of attachment and that higher levels of affection would lead to higher odds of clinging as opposed to avoidance. All of these effects would be exacerbated by a positive home environment compared with a negative home environment. Thus, the home environment was thought to moderate the impact of affection on the odds of exhibiting one form of attachment relative to another. The measure of affection was mean centered prior to analysis.

The data were analyzed using the multinomial regression program in SPSS, with secure attachment specified as the baseline group. The analysis yielded two equations, one equation comparing secure attachment to clinging and a second equation comparing secure attachment to avoidance. Using formulas presented in Agresti (1996), it is possible to algebraically derive the coefficients for the comparison of clinging versus avoidance from the above two equations. However, one can also compute the coefficients for this comparison by changing the baseline group and then rerunning the analysis on the computer. The latter strategy has the advantage of yielding estimated standard errors, significance tests, and confidence intervals for the predictors in the clinging versus avoidance comparison. Table 9 presents the results

TABLE 9
Logistic Coefficients for Multicategory Outcome Variables

	Predictor	Logistic Coefficient	Exponent of Coefficient	95% Lower Limit	95% Upper Limit	p Value
Secure vs. avoidance	Home (H)	1.378	3.966	2.452	6.416	<0.001
	Affection (A)	0.961	2.615	2.049	3.336	<0.001
	H * A	0.731	2.078	1.473	2.932	<0.001
	Intercept	−1.012				
Clinging vs. avoidance	Home (H)	0.501	1.651	1.044	2.611	0.032
	Affection (A)	0.549	1.731	1.361	2.202	<0.001
	H * A	0.363	1.438	1.058	1.953	0.020
	Intercept	−0.626				
Secure vs. clinging	Home (H)	0.876	2.402	1.462	3.946	<0.001
	Affection (A)	0.413	1.511	1.232	1.852	<0.001
	H * A	0.368	1.445	1.091	1.915	0.010
	Intercept	−0.386				

for the three equations. Each equation is interpreted using the same framework presented in Chapter 3 for the case of a categorical moderator variable and a continuous focal independent variable. For the equation focused on secure attachment (scored 1) versus avoidance (scored 0), the exponent of the coefficient for affection was 2.615. This is the multiplying factor by which the odds of secure attachment (relative to avoidance) changes given a 1-unit change in affection when the home environment is negative. If we reversed the dummy coding for home environment so that 1 = negative and 0 = positive, recalculate the product term, and then rerun the analysis, we would find that the exponent of the coefficient for affection is 5.434. This is the multiplying factor by which the odds of secure attachment (relative to avoidance) changes given a 1-unit change in affection when the home environment is positive. The ratio of these two multiplying factors is 5.434/2.615 = 2.078, which is the value of the exponent for the product term. Because the confidence interval for the product term does not contain the value of 1.0, the discrepancy between the two multiplying factors for the positive versus negative home environment is statistically significant. The data for this equation are consistent with the researcher's hypothesis. We leave it as an exercise for the reader to interpret the remaining two equations in Table 9. For elaboration of the analysis of multicategory outcome variables, see Long (1997).

In sum, the logistic model is often used to analyze dichotomous outcome variables, but it also forms the basis for the analysis of multicategory outcome variables. This includes the analysis of ordinal outcomes and multilevel qualitative outcomes. The basic concepts presented in Chapters 1 through 4 can be readily extended to the interpretation of product terms in such models.

6. ADDITIONAL CONSIDERATIONS

This chapter addresses selected issues in interaction analysis that complement the material in previous chapters. We consider first tabular and graphical methods that will assist in the presentation of interaction effects. We then discuss how to calculate confidence intervals of the exponents of coefficients if such intervals are not provided in computer software and how to calculate the coefficient for a focal variable at any value of a moderator variable from a single equation. We next discuss limiting forms of traditional interaction analysis and methods for expanding the type of interaction modeled. Finally, we consider issues related to the partialling of component terms, the analysis of multiple interactions, multicollinearity, theory trimming, confounded configurations, and computer software.

Methods of Presenting Interaction Effects

Interaction effects often are difficult for readers of reports to conceptualize. Explicit identification of the role of each variable as either a focal independent variable or a moderator variable is helpful. The coefficients of the logistic equation contain all of the core information necessary to interpret interactions. However, it may be useful if the coefficients are augmented with tables or graphs. The present section discusses strategies for presenting the results of interactive logistic models beyond mere presentation of the coefficients and/or their exponents.

When the interaction of interest involves only qualitative variables, then tables of the form of Table 4 make interpretation easier. The predicted odds are presented within the cells of the table, with the focal independent variable defining the rows and the moderator variable defining the columns of the table. The odds ratio for the relevant levels of the focal independent variable is presented beneath each column. If a three-way interaction is reported, the ratio of the odds ratios can be reported beneath these entries, as in Table 4. If the focal independent variable has more than two levels, then sub-tables may be required to present all the single degree of freedom interaction contrasts of interest. Table 10 presents an example for a 3×3 interaction that addresses all pairwise interaction contrasts at each level of the moderator variable. In this table, ethnicity is the focal independent variable and geographic location is the moderator variable. Confidence intervals are omitted for the sake of simplicity, but these normally would be presented in parentheses next to each entry. Section b shows how the predicted odds ratio for any two groups of the focal independent variable (ethnicity) changes as a function of the values of the moderator variable (geographic location). For three-way interactions, columns of the moderator variables are expanded to incorporate both moderators, as in Table 4. If a covariate is included in the analysis, then the predicted odds in the tables are calculated holding the covariate constant at a theoretically meaningful value (e.g., its sample mean).

For interactions between qualitative and quantitative/continuous variables where the quantitative variable, X, is the focal independent variable, it may be useful to supplement the numerical information with a graph depicting the predicted log odds across the values of X for each of the groups defined by the moderator variable. In practice, one could plot either the predicted odds, the predicted log odds, or the predicted probabilities and each would provide visual perspectives on the dynamics that are operating. The most straightforward plots are those using the predicted log odds because all of the functions are linear in form and an interaction is characterized by nonparallel lines (as in standard ordinary least squares regression and in analysis of variance). However, such plots require that the reader have an intuitive sense of the property of log odds, which comes with experience with these types of methods. Figure 1 plots the predicted log odds for the three ethnic groups from the example in Chapter 2, in which ethnicity was the moderator variable and years of education was the focal independent variable. The nonparallel slopes are indicative of the interaction and the degree of nonparallelness gives some appreciation of the magnitude of the interaction.

In the case of a three-way interaction, one can employ the same graphical device but with side-by-side plots in which separate graphs are presented for each level of the second-order moderator variable.

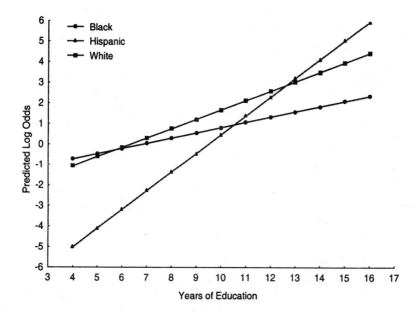

Figure 1. Example of a Plot for a Quantitative/Continuous Focal Independent Variable and a Qualitative Moderator Variable: Two-Way Interaction

Figure 2 presents an example in which the predicted log odds of parent attendance at a workshop on adolescent drug use is plotted as a function of concern for drug use (the quantitative/continuous focal independent variable), employment status (the first-order moderator variable), and the number of choices of workshops made available to the parent (the second-order moderator variable), holding social class constant at its sample mean value.

For cases in which the qualitative variable is the focal independent variable and the quantitative/continuous variable is the moderator variable, a table having the format of Table 10 can be used to illustrate the interaction effect. Because the moderator variable has many values, one typically chooses two or three illustrative values at which to generate the predicted odds. For example, one might present a table of predicted odds and odds ratios when the quantitative moderator variable is equal to a "low" value (such as 1 standard deviation below its mean), a "medium" value (such as at its mean), and a "high" value (such as 1 standard deviation above its mean).

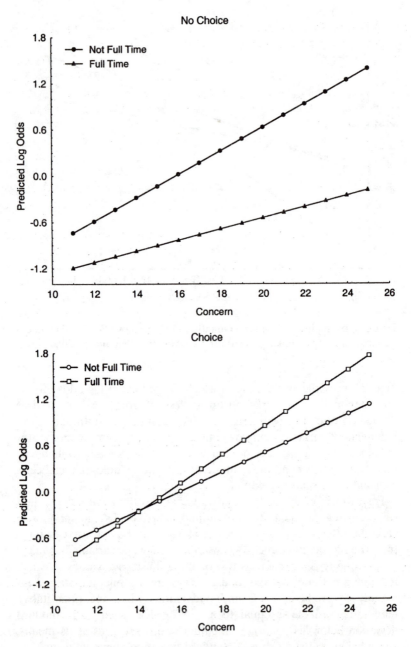

Figure 2. Example of a Plot for a Quantitative/Continuous Focal Independent Variable and a Qualitative Moderator Variable: Three-Way Interaction

TABLE 10
Presentation of a 3 × 3 Interaction

	Urban	Suburban	Rural
a. Predicted Odds			
Black	2.00	3.00	4.00
Hispanic	4.00	3.00	2.00
White	6.00	6.00	6.00
b. Odds Ratios			
Black/Hispanic	0.50	1.00	2.00
Black/White	0.33	0.50	0.67
Hispanic/White	0.67	0.50	0.33

For interactions involving two quantitative/continuous variables, one can adapt the above strategies to convey a sense of the interaction. As noted earlier, one can supplement the numerical information with plots of either the predicted log odds, predicted odds, or predicted probabilities of the outcome variable across the values of the focal independent variable at each level of the moderator variable. However, in this case, such a plot is not feasible because the moderator variable has too many values. Instead, one can select two or three illustrative values of the moderator variable and use these in the plot. For example, one could select a low, medium, and high score on the moderator variable to illustrate the curves. Figure 3 presents an example of such a plot for the predicted log odds of taking an HIV test as a function of the perceived risk of contracting HIV (the focal independent variable) and the perceived severity of the consequences of contracting HIV (the moderator variable). This plot was generated by calculating the logistic equation for the scenario where none of the variables were subjected to a transformation (i.e., using the original raw scores). The resulting equation was then used to generate predicted log odds across the risk variable where a value for severity was substituted into the equation using either a low, a medium, or a high score on severity. Three-way interactions can be presented using this same strategy, but choosing two or three values of theoretical interest on the second-order moderator variable and then using side-by-side plots.

An alternative to these traditional plots is three-dimensional plots of response surfaces. Such methods are discussed in Cook and Weisberg (1995).

58

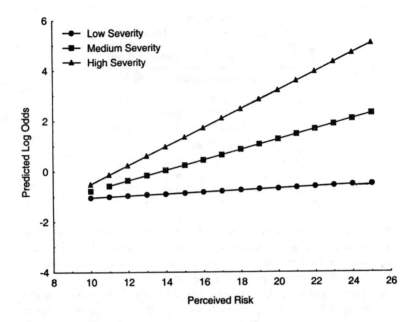

Figure 3. Example of a Plot for a Two Quantitative/Continuous Predictors: Two-Way Interaction

Calculating Confidence Intervals

Some computer packages provide estimated standard errors for the logistic coefficients but do not provide the confidence intervals for the exponents of the coefficients. These can be derived from the provided information (assuming that the sample size is sufficiently large for asymptotic theory to hold). To calculate the confidence interval, select a critical value from a standardized normal distribution. For a 95% confidence interval, this is $Z_{critical} = 1.96$. Multiply this value by the estimated standard error of the logistic coefficient in question. Subtract this product from the logistic coefficient to obtain the lower limit of the confidence interval for the coefficient and add this product to the logistic coefficient to obtain the upper limit of the confidence interval for the coefficient. Finally, calculate the exponents of the lower and upper limits to obtain the confidence interval for the exponent of the coefficient.

Calculating Coefficients of Focal Independent Variables at Different Moderator Values

In previous chapters, coefficients for the focal independent variable were calculated at different values of the moderator variable by either transforming the quantitative/continuous predictor or by redefining the reference group of a qualitative predictor and then rerunning the logistic analysis on the computer. This approach, though cumbersome, has the advantage of producing confidence intervals for all of the parameters of interest. Such confidence intervals are not readily calculated by hand [see Hosmer & Lemeshow (1989), for relevant formulas]. Occasions may arise where one wishes to calculate the coefficients from the initial equation without generating confidence intervals and without redoing the analyses with transformed variables. This section describes how to do so.

Consider the case in which X is the focal independent variable and Z is the moderator variable in the equation

$$\text{logit}(\pi) = \alpha + \beta_1 X + \beta_2 Z + \beta_3 XZ. \qquad [8]$$

We want to determine the coefficient for X at some value of Z. We first isolate all terms on the right-hand side of the equation that contain X,

$$\beta_1 X + \beta_3 XZ,$$

and then factor out the X,

$$X(\beta_1 + \beta_3 Z),$$

which yields the coefficient for X at any value of Z, namely,

$$\beta \text{ for } X \text{ at } Z = \beta_1 + \beta_3 Z. \qquad [9]$$

For example, in Equation 8, if $\beta_1 = 1.2$ and $\beta_3 = 0.05$, then the logistic coefficient for X when $Z = 2$ is $1.2 + (0.05)(2) = 1.30$. Note that when $Z = 0$, the value of the coefficient in Equation 9 is β_1, which underscores the point that β_1 is conditioned on Z being 0. If X and Z are dummy variables, the logic of Equation 9 holds but is focused only on the relevant dummy variables. For example, suppose

X has two dummy variables and Z has two dummy variables, yielding the following:

$$\text{logit}(\pi) = \alpha + \beta_1 D_{X1} + \beta_2 D_{X2} + \beta_3 D_{Z1} + \beta_4 D_{Z2} + \beta_5 D_{X1} D_{Z1}$$
$$+ \beta_6 D_{X1} D_{Z2} + \beta_7 D_{X2} D_{Z1} + \beta_8 D_{X2} D_{Z2}.$$

Suppose we want to isolate the odds ratio for the group scored 1 on D_{X1} versus the reference group on X for the case in which $D_{Z1} = 1$ and $D_{Z2} = 1$. We first isolate only the terms and coefficients that directly involve D_{X1},

$$\beta_1 D_{X1} + \beta_5 D_{X1} D_{Z1} + \beta_6 D_{X1} D_{Z2},$$

and factor out D_{X1} to yield

$$D_{X1}(\beta_1 + \beta_5 D_{Z1} + \beta_6 D_{Z2})$$

so that

$$\beta \text{ for } D_{X1} \text{ at } D_{Z1} \text{ and } D_{Z2} = \beta_1 + \beta_5 D_{Z1} + \beta_6 D_{Z2}.$$

For the case in which $\beta_1 = 0.2$, $\beta_5 = 0.3$, $\beta_6 = 0.4$, and $D_{Z1} = 1$ and $D_{Z2} = 1$, the coefficient for D_{X1} is $[0.2 + (0.3)(1) + (0.4)(1)] = 0.9$.

Equations for three-way interactions use the same logic. In the case of three continuous predictors, X, Q, and Z, the traditional interaction equation is

$$\text{logit}(\pi) = \alpha + \beta_1 X + \beta_2 Q + \beta_3 Z + \beta_4 XQ$$
$$+ \beta_5 XZ + \beta_6 QZ + \beta_7 XQZ.$$

The coefficient for X at a given combination of scores on Q and Z is

$$\beta \text{ for } X \text{ at } Q \text{ and } Z = \beta_1 + \beta_4 Q + \beta_5 Z + \beta_7 QZ$$

and the coefficient for XQ at a given value of Z is

$$\beta \text{ for } XQ \text{ at } Z = \beta_4 + \beta_7 Z.$$

The Bilinear Nature of Interactions for Continuous/Quantitative Variables

When a quantitative/continuous variable is part of an interaction, it is important to keep in mind that the use of product terms as described in earlier chapters tests only for an interaction that has a specific form, namely a bilinear interaction for the log odds. Other forms of interaction may be operating and exploratory analyses should routinely be performed to ensure that the correct type of interaction is being modeled. As an example, consider Figure 4 which plots the log odds of an outcome variable as a function of a quantitative/continuous focal independent variable, X, for two groups. An interactive logistic model assumes that for both groups, the log odds are a linear function of X and the nature of the interaction is characterized by nonparallel lines. However, this is not the case for these data. For one group, the

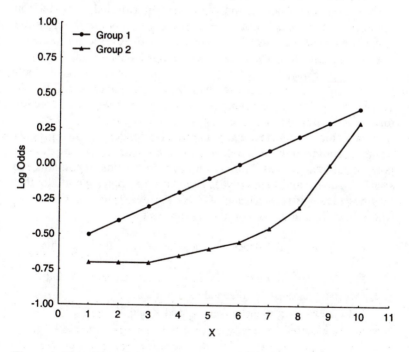

Figure 4. Plot of Log Odds as a Function of a Continuous Predictor for Two Groups

log odds are indeed a linear function of X, but for the other group the log odds are a nonlinear function of X. In this case, the logistic model with product terms as described in this monograph is not appropriate because it represents a misspecified model.

In the case of two quantitative/continuous variables, the classic product term approach reflects a narrowly defined but probably widely applicable interaction form. As noted in Chapter 1, if X is the focal independent variable and Z is the moderator variable, the product term approach models the logistic coefficient for X as a linear function of Z. It is possible that the logistic coefficient of X changes as a nonlinear function of Z and if this is the case, the traditional product term approach represents a misspecified model. A crude but sometimes informative way to explore this issue is to use a variant of bandwidth regression (Hamilton, 1992). In this approach, the moderator variable is grouped into 5 to 10 equal-sized, ordered categories. The mean or median Z is calculated for each group and a logistic analysis regressing the outcome onto X is performed separately on each group. Examination of the logistic coefficients for X across the 5 to 10 groups should reveal a trend whereby the coefficient increases or decreases as a roughly linear function of the mean or median of Z. Stated another way, if one plots from such an analysis the logistic coefficients against the mean (or median) Z values, a linear trend should be evident. If this is not the case, then a more complex interaction form may be needed.

Such complex interactions often can be modeled using product terms in conjunction with polynomial terms. For an introduction to polynomial analysis with interaction terms in multiple regression, see Jaccard, Turrisi, and Wan (1990). The steps for applying a model that assumes the logistic coefficient for X is a quadratic function of Z, where both X and Z are continuous, are as follows:

1. Identify the focal independent variable, X, and the moderator variable, Z.
2. Make any desired transformations (e.g., mean center) on X and Z.
3. Calculate the square of the moderator variable, Z^2.
4. Calculate product terms between X and Z and X and Z^2.
5. Fit the equation: $\text{logit}(\pi) = \alpha + \beta_1 X + \beta_2 Z + \beta_3 Z^2 + \beta_4 XZ + \beta_5 XZ^2$.

A hierarchical test for improvement in model fit by adding the XZ^2 term indicates if the quadratic interaction effect is nontrivial. The coefficient for X at a given value of Z is defined by $\beta_1 + \beta_4 Z + \beta_5 Z^2$. The coefficient β_1 is the coefficient for X when $Z = 0$. One can transform Z (in Step 2 above) so that a score of zero on the transformed variable takes on a theoretically meaningful value to isolate the relevant coefficient and confidence interval for the coefficient for X at a given value of Z.

For the case involving a qualitative and continuous variable as depicted in Figure 4, assume that Z is a dummy variable scored with 1's and 0's to represent group membership. In this case, the log odds as a function of the continuous focal independent variable, X, is nonlinear for at least one of the groups. Fit the following model: $\text{logit}(\pi) = \alpha + \beta_1 X + \beta_2 Z + \beta_3 X^2 + \beta_4 XZ + \beta_5 X^2 Z$. The effect of X on $\text{logit}(\pi)$ when $Z = 0$ is reflected by the quadratic model $\alpha + \beta_1 X + \beta_3 X^2$ within this equation. To find the effect of X when $Z = 1$, recode Z by reverse coding it, recalculate the product terms, and rerun the computer program, again focusing on $\alpha + \beta_1 X + \beta_3 X^2$.

Partialling the Component Terms

It is sometimes stated that the product terms in logistic equations represent interaction effects. By and of themselves, the product terms reflect an amalgamation of main effects and interactions. In general, it is only when the component parts of the product term are included in the equation along with the product term that the orderly relationships described in this monograph emerge (coupled with an unconstrained intercept term). It is possible to model interactions in ways that lead one to exclude one or more of the component parts of the product term, but this typically represents interactions of a different form from those considered in this monograph.

Multiple Interaction Effects

Consider a case in which an investigator desires to model a dichotomous outcome, Y, as a function of three continuous predictors, X, Q, and Z. The researcher does not expect a three-way interaction between the predictors but wants to evaluate all possible two-way interactions. There are multiple strategies that might be used. Some analysts perform a "chunk" test in which the fit of a model with all (two-way) interaction terms included is contrasted with the fit of a model with none of the interaction terms; i.e., the interactions are tested as a chunk (Kleinbaum, 1992). If the difference in fit of the two models is trivial, then this suggests that none of the interaction terms are necessary and they are dropped from the model. If application of the chunk test reveals a nontrivial difference in model fit, then this suggests that at least one interaction term is important to retain. At this point, a hierarchical backward elimination strategy is used, comparing the fit of a model that includes all of the interaction terms versus the fit of a model that drops a particular term(s) of interest. For example, if one is interested in evaluating the XZ interaction, one would compare the fit of the model

$$\text{logit}(\pi) = \alpha + \beta_1 Q + \beta_2 X + \beta_3 Z + \beta_4 QX + \beta_5 QZ + \beta_6 XZ$$

with the fit of the model

$$\text{logit}(\pi) = \alpha + \beta_1 Q + \beta_2 X + \beta_3 Z + \beta_4 QX + \beta_5 QZ.$$

If the difference in fit between the models is trivial, then this suggests that the XZ term can be eliminated. However, if the difference in the fit of the model is nontrivial, then the term should be retained.

Some analysts systematically evaluate each interaction term in this fashion. Other analysts choose one term to focus on first, and if that term is eliminated, evaluate the remaining interaction terms with the previously eliminated term(s) expunged from the model. For example, if we tested XZ first for possible elimination and ultimately decided to drop it from the model, then the evaluation of QZ would focus on a backward elimination test where XZ was not present in the model; i.e., we would evaluate

$$\text{logit}(\pi) = \alpha + \beta_1 Q + \beta_2 X + \beta_3 Z + \beta_4 QX + \beta_5 QZ$$

versus

$$\text{logit}(\pi) = \alpha + \beta_1 Q + \beta_2 X + \beta_3 Z + \beta_4 QX.$$

The choice of which term to evaluate first for possible elimination is sometimes based on theoretical criteria, on whichever term has the largest p value associated with its logistic coefficient in the full equation, or on both.

In multiple interaction scenarios, there are many model-fitting criteria that can be invoked for the trimming of terms and controversy exists about the advisability of each. Consideration of the relevant issues is beyond the scope of this monograph. Interested readers are referred to Bishop, Feinberg, and Holland (1975), Hosmer and Lemeshow (1989), and Jaccard (1998) for a discussion of germane issues. The reader should be forewarned that seeming "anomalies" can occur as multiple interaction terms of the same order are considered. For example, the chunk test might indicate that at least one of the product terms should be retained in the model, but the evaluation of each individual term may suggest that each term can be eliminated from the model. Or, the results of the individual tests of one term may suggest that the term be retained and that all others be eliminated, but when the others are eliminated, the candidate for retention becomes nonsignificant and of trivial predictive value. How one deals with these scenarios depends on the theoretical questions being addressed, one's overarching statistical framework (e.g., null hypothesis testing, magnitude estimation, or interval estimation), and the patterning of the data. In most analytic situations, the choice of terms to trim will be straightforward and noncontroversial, but this is not always the case.

When two separate interaction terms are included in the logistic equation (e.g., for three continuous predictors, Q, X and Z, and both XZ and QZ are retained in the equation but no other interaction terms are), then the coefficient for a given interaction term is interpreted as described in previous chapters, but with the proviso that the other two-way interactions (as well as all other covariates) are statistically held constant. The coefficient for any lower order term is conditional to the other variables in all product terms that it is involved with being zero.

Multicollinearity

Some researchers are wary of interaction analysis with product terms because the product term often is highly correlated with the component parts used to define the product term. If XZ is highly correlated with either X, Z, or both, the fear is that the evaluation of the interaction effect will be undermined due to classic problems of multicollinearity. This generally will not be the case unless the multicollinearity with the product term is so high (e.g., 0.98 or greater) that it disrupts the computer algorithm designed to isolate the relevant standard errors. A sense that collinearity with XZ is nonproblematic is indicated by the fact that the wide range of transformations for continuous predictors discussed in previous chapters will usually alter the correlation between XZ and its component parts, but will have no effect on the value of the logistic coefficient for the product term, its estimated standard error, or the critical ratio testing its statistical significance. If collinearity was crucial, then the coefficient and its estimated standard error would not remain invariant as the correlation between XZ and its component parts changes. For a discussion of the rationale of this phenomenon, see Jaccard, Turrisi, and Wan (1990). High collinearity between X and Z (i.e., the component parts), on the other hand, can lead to serious problems.

Model Selection and Trimming

In many applications in the social sciences, researchers have well-defined hypotheses that dictate a statistical model for purposes of testing those hypotheses. For example, one might posit an interaction between gender of an adolescent and employment status of the mother of the adolescent and then test a model that explicitly explores all aspects of this interaction. In other situations, analysts approach their research questions by exploring the utility of a set of predictors with an eye toward specifying a parsimonious prediction equation that adequately accounts for the outcome in question. A common strategy is to include a set of predictors that are deemed theoretically relevant and then to "trim" the model by eliminating any predictors that are statistically nonsignificant or whose coefficients are so close to zero that they are deemed trivial in magnitude and, hence, ignorable. Such trimming not only yields a more parsimonious model but also increases the statistical power of the analysis. Trimming variables, especially if they are part of a product term, must be done with care because eliminating variables that have nonzero coefficients can introduce bias into the model, thereby undermining interpretation of the coefficients. Trimming several variables, each of which might have near zero and nonsignificant effects, can have the effect of introducing bias when the variables are trimmed as a collective. Nonsignificant effects for a predictor may be due to low power, with the result that an important (but statistically nonsignificant) variable is trimmed, yielding bias that is consequential rather than inconsequential. In general, trimming potentially theoretically meaningful variables is not advisable unless one is quite certain that the coefficient for the variable is near zero, that the variable is inconsequential, and that trimming will not introduce misspecification error. The advantage of trimming is that one typically saves a single degree of freedom and gains a more parsimonious model. The disadvantage of trimming is that model misspecification can result, thereby undermining interpretation of the coefficients within the model. When sample sizes are large, the trivial gain in power by saving a few degrees of freedom does not outweigh the potentially serious problems that can derive from model misspecification, making trimming a practice that should be enacted with caution.

Transformations

Throughout this monograph, we relied on transformations of the predictor variables to force the parameters of the logistic models to take on meaningful values. Often, we analyzed the same equation but under different transformations to assist us in extracting useful information or vantage points on the data. These transformations, though computationally inelegant, are useful because they yield estimated standard errors and confidence intervals that would otherwise be cumbersome to calculate for the novice. These strategies can also be used in traditional ordinary least squares regression as the general principles governing transformations developed here apply in that case as well. The approach can also be used to effectively analyze four-way and five-way interactions. One must simply keep in mind the conditional nature of the coefficients and what values the transformations target [see the rules governing such conditional relations described in the appendix of Jaccard (1998)]. Care must be taken in the application of the approach in the presence of missing data, because the regularities may be altered if strategies other than listwise deletion or value imputation are used.

Confounded Interactions

Interaction effects may be confounded with other types of effects and care must be taken to ensure that the tested model is not misspecified. For example, the data may be the result of a generating process that results from a curvilinear relationship between logit (") and X, but when an interaction model is fit to the data using X and Z as predictors, a significant interaction effect is observed. Some analysts suggest testing for such curvilinear effects before pursuing interaction analysis, if they make theoretical sense. Obviously, one must think carefully about the possible models that can account for data and then explore these models. One important form of confounding in interaction analysis for logistic models has been identified by Allison (1999b). The confounding involves residual variation (more specifically, unobserved heterogeneity) and can produce group differences in logistic coefficients when no such differences are implied by the underlying causal structure. Allison (1999b) explicates the nature of the confound, strategies for testing its presence, and methods of analysis given violations of the assumption of residual homogeneity. The pervasiveness of the confound in research applications is not known and may or may not be problematic depending on a wide array of considerations.

Computer Software

Interaction analyses described in this monograph are easily implemented in computer programs by calculating the relevant product terms and entering them directly into the logistic regression programs with other relevant covariates or predictors. Some programs offer shortcuts for the calculation of product terms. For example, S Plus permits the user to specify an interaction between terms using simple point and click procedures and then the program generates the relevant product terms internally. In the case of categorical predictors, the relevant dummy variables are automatically generated and product terms formed accordingly. In using such programs, one must be careful to determine what type of dummy codes are generated by the program (e.g., dummy coding or effect coding) and which group is defined as the reference group. Also, with multicategory regression models, one must be careful to ensure that the desired model is being estimated because a wide variety of models exist and there is variability with respect to the default model imposed. In addition, programs differ in the default definition of the baseline group.

NOTES

1. On a hand calculator, the key often labeled e^x will calculate the exponent of the value entered on the calculator.

2. There also are models that do not rely on the logit function.

REFERENCES

AGRESTI, A. (1996) *An Introduction to Categorical Data Analysis*. New York: Wiley.

ALLISON, P. (1999a) Comparing Logit and Probit Coefficients Across Groups. *Sociological Methods and Research*, 28, 186–208.

ALLISON, P. (1999b) *Logistic Regression Using the SAS System: Theory and Application*. Cary, NC: SAS Institute.

BISHOP, Y. M., Feinberg, S., & Holland, P. W. (1975) *Discrete Multivariate Analysis: Theory and Practice*. Cambridge, MA: MIT Press.

COOK, R. D., & Weisberg, S. (1995) *An Introduction to Regression Graphics*. New York: Wiley.

HARDY, K. (1993) *Regression with Dummy Variables*. Sage University Papers Series on Quantitative Applications in the Social Sciences, 07-93. Thousand Oaks, CA: Sage.

HAMILTON, L. C. (1992) *Regression with Graphics: A Second Course in Applied Statistics*. Belmont, CA: Brooks Cole.

HOSMER, D. W., & Lemeshow, S. (1989) *Applied Logistic Regression*. New York: Wiley.

JACCARD, J. (1998) *Interaction Effects in Factorial Analysis of Variance*. Sage University Papers Series on Quantitative Applications in the Social Sciences, 07-118. Thousand Oaks, CA: Sage.

JACCARD, J., & Wan, C.K. (1996) *LISREL Analyses of Interaction Effects in Multiple Regression*. Sage University Papers Series on Quantitative Applications in the Social Sciences, 07-114. Thousand Oaks, CA: Sage.

JACCARD, J., Turrisi, R., & Wan, C. (1990) *Interaction Effects in Multiple Regression*. Sage University Papers Series on Quantitative Applications in the Social Sciences, 07-72. Thousand Oaks, CA: Sage.

KIRK, R. (1995) *Experimental Design: Procedures for the Behavioral Sciences*. Pacific Grove, CA: Brooks-Cole.

KLEINBAUM, D. G. (1992) *Logistic Regression: A Self Learning Text*. New York: Springer.

LONG, S. (1997) *Regression Models for Categorical and Limited Dependent Variables*. Thousand Oaks, CA: Sage.

MAGIDSON, J. (1998) *Goldminer 2.0*. Chicago: SPSS.

MAXWELL, S., & Delaney, H. (1990) *Designing Experiments and Analyzing Data: A Model Comparison Approach*. Belmont, CA: Wadsworth.

MCCULLAGH, P., & Nelder, J. A. (1989) *Generalized Linear Models*. London: Chapman and Hall.

MENARD, S. (1995) *Applied Logistic Regression Analysis*. Sage University Papers Series on Quantitative Applications in the Social Sciences, 07-106. Thousand Oaks, CA: Sage.

ABOUT THE AUTHOR

JAMES JACCARD is a Distinguished Professor of Psychology at the University of Albany, State University of New York. His primary research interests are in the areas of the psychology of population dynamics and adolescent risk behavior, with an emphasis on adolescent unintended pregnancy and adolescent drunk driving. His work has focused on family based approaches to dealing with adolescent problem behaviors. He has authored three other monographs on interaction effects in the Sage series.